THE PIFCO
FOOD
PROCESSOR
COOKBOOK
MARY MORRIS ADRIENNE KATZ

THE PIFCO
FOOD
PROCESSOR
COOKBOOK
MARY MORRIS ADRIENNE KATZ

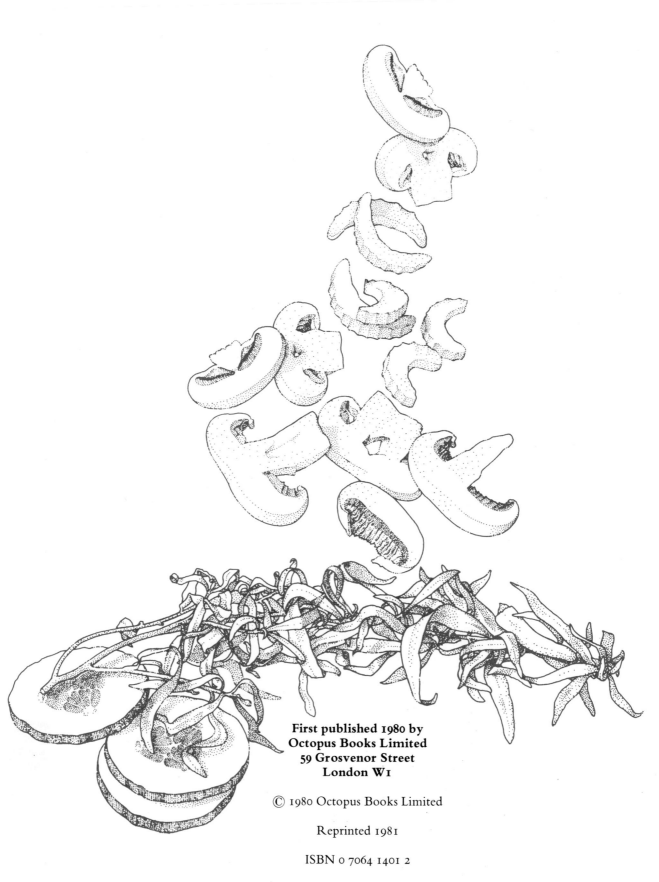

First published 1980 by
Octopus Books Limited
59 Grosvenor Street
London W1

© 1980 Octopus Books Limited

Reprinted 1981

ISBN 0 7064 1401 2

Produced by Mandarin Publishers Limited
22a Westlands Road
Quarry Bay, Hong Kong

Printed in Hong Kong

CONTENTS

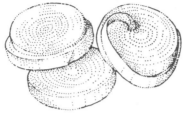

INTRODUCTION

What is a food processor? It is a neat, compact yet very powerful machine that will become your extra right-hand in an amazing number of kitchen tasks, in a very short time.

What does it do? Time consuming and repetitive chores in food preparation are completed in seconds, and are enjoyable to do too! This machine will mix, knead, chop, mince, purée, combine, cream, blend, slice, shred and grate simply with a change of blade or disc.

With a food processor in the kitchen you will never be caught short when unexpected visitors drop in. All types of quick meals can be speedily prepared then put in the oven to cook while you are greeting the visitors.

At busy times of the year the processor can be used to help with the workload. At Christmas time and during holidays, particularly if hungry members of the family are present, the machine will prepare soups, main meals, vegetables and biscuits (cookies) in next to no time.

If you have had your processor for awhile and want to know how to use it to the full extent, the chapter on Short Cut Ingredients and Multiple Meals will help. As well as giving ideas and suggestions for preparing ingredients that are always used it gives suggestions for 'chain cooking', which takes advantage of gluts of food.

A food processor is one of the most useful additions to a kitchen and will relieve you of tiring and time-consuming chores. Once you have had your machine for awhile, you will wonder how you ever managed without it!

USING A FOOD PROCESSOR

A food processor is a recent addition to the electrical range of kitchen appliances. It is easily put together, simple to use and will change the way you cook.

KNOW YOUR MACHINE
The few basic parts consist of the *motor base* and the *bowl* with its *lid*, through which the food is fed into the bowl by a *pusher*. As the processor takes up such a small amount of bench space have it standing ready on the workbench all the time. This is much easier than bending to the cupboard every time you want to use the machine.

The attachments are:
THE METAL BLADE. This is the most commonly used tool – used for chopping, mincing, mixing, making pastry, kneading dough and to purée. Cut the ingredients into small pieces before putting into the feed tube, or bowl, particularly if using hard substances.

If you start with the food cut into equal sized pieces, you will get a more even end result, whether for mincing (grinding) meat or chopping onions. Always process by turning the machine on and off. When using pulse action check the size of the processed food through the lid.

Solid chunks are reduced to little pieces so quickly that if you are not alert they will be reduced even further to a cream or purée.
THE SLICING DISC cuts even slices of raw vegetables, fruits, sausages and cheese.
THE GRATING DISC will grate cheese, fruit, vegetables, chocolate and nuts.
THE PLASTIC BLADE is used for mixing, beating and whipping and to combine sauces.
A SPATULA is used for scraping down the bowl and the blades.

The simplicity of operating food processors is a boon to those among us who are not at all mechanical minded; there is no complicated assembly or tightening of screws and bolts. Simply select the blade or disc of your choice and fit its white cylinder onto the motor drive shaft in the centre of the bowl. Your processor is now ready to use.

ASSEMBLY

MOTOR BASE AND BOWL. With the brown column and switches nearest you, hold the handle of the bowl in your right hand. Lower it onto the power drive shaft and turn it to lock onto the guide bumps on the base. (These are located at 9 o'clock and 3 o'clock in relation to the switch column.)

Make certain the guide bumps are exactly in the slots provided on the bowl.

BLADE. Lower the blade you have chosen onto the power drive shaft and rotate until it drops down. The slicing and grating discs have white plastic cylinders which fit onto the shaft; their blades will be just below the top of the bowl. The metal and plastic blades settle lower down inside the bowl.

LID. Grasp the lid by the feed tube with your right hand and place onto the bowl.

Turn it so that the notch nearest the word 'LOCK' printed on the lid is between the bowl handle and the switch column. Then, holding the feed tube, simply turn in the direction of the arrow, and lock by bringing the indicating ridge to the centre of the brown switch column.

The machine is ready for action.

Switches
ON for processing for longer periods.
PULSE for on/off pulse action.

Food is generally fed into the bowl through the tube and is pushed down by the pusher when using the grating or slicing disc. Pressure on this affects the size of the slice or grate. Always use the pusher, *never* your fingers, and take care when handling the blades not to cut yourself. For most processing, the machine is turned on as the food is added.

To *release the lid* turn anticlockwise, holding the feed tube in right hand.

Release the bowl by pushing anticlockwise with the handle.

Liquids
When handling liquids always watch the 'max liquid level guide' marked on the side of the bowl. If your processor does not have a maximum liquid level, do not fill above the level of the central spindle.

When removing the bowl with liquid in it, do not lift out the blade; simply lift the entire bowl and blade with the handle, and pour the liquid into a bowl.

Batches
Always process food in small batches rather than overfill the bowl.

When chopping hard or heavy foods CUT INTO CUBES and process in bursts, using the pulse action switch.

CARE OF THE MACHINE

Take care not to cut your fingers on the extremely sharp surfaces of the blades. Hold the plastic area of the disc or blade and rinse under hot water, and if necessary, brush down with a washing brush and dishwashing liquid. Dry. If you wash the sharp metal blade in soapy water, always drain the water out before feeling for the blade in the suds. You may cut yourself.

The bowl and its lid are dishwasherproof and will stand normal washing up water temperature without damage. Do not use scourers, steel wool or scouring powder to clean the bowl as they will scratch the surface. The pusher should be rinsed in the sink and left to dry. Wipe the motor base with a damp cloth – DO NOT IMMERSE IN WATER.

WHAT A FOOD PROCESSOR WILL NOT DO

The processor will purée but not liquify. It will not incorporate air into egg whites or cream to produce meringue mixtures or whipped cream. The machine will not grind coffee beans.

The capacity of any machine is limited and a food processor is no exception. Food should be processed in batches and you must take care not to overload the machine. The manufacturers' instruction leaflet will tell you how much to process at one time.

Apart from these few exceptions, the abilities of a food processor are endless. The excitement it generates will encourage you to experiment and adjust your recipes again and again.

HOW TO GET THE BEST OUT OF THIS MACHINE

A few experiments will illustrate how quickly substantial chunks of meat are reduced to tiny minced (ground) pieces. If you watch closely through the lid you will be able to gauge how many seconds you need to process the meat to the desired consistency. Take care, as with the high speed and powerful blades some foods are puréed before you know it!

This machine will simplify all chopping, slicing and grating of vegetables, fruits, meats, nuts and cheese. It will also emulsify delicate sauces – such as mayonnaise and béarnaise, cream butter and sugar, or combine ingredients for a steak tartare. It will pulverise nuts to make delicious butters, for example your own homemade peanut butter. A food processor is the answer if you have never been any good at pastry making; beautiful, almost foolproof, pastries are produced in seconds.

With the speed and power of a food processor, many new and exciting possibilities for cooking will open up as you become experienced in using the machine.

SOUPS AND STARTERS

Most people like starters and it is a pleasant way to begin the meal. Only a small portion is needed and it whets the appetite for what is to follow, whether a family meal, weekend lunch or a special dinner.

Soups are ideal for all occasions and as they usually involve quite a bit of chopping and perhaps puréeing, your food processsor can do all the hard work and reduce the preparation time.

Starters can be served hot or cold; can be made from vegetables, meat or fish; and can be eaten with a fork and knife or the fingers. A platter of crisp, raw vegetables served with homemade garlic-flavoured mayonnaise can be prepared in minutes with the processor slicing the vegetables and making the mayonnaise (page 48). Pâté is another favourite starter that can also double as a light meal or turn into another starter. The Smoked Mackerel Pâté (page 24) can be served with toast and butter or can be piped into baked choux pastry to become Smoked Mackerel Éclairs (page 22).

Meals need a variety of tastes, textures and colours to be satisfying, and a soup or starter is a good way to begin. Plan the remainder of the meal to contrast and complement the starter, using your processor to produce smooth or coarse textured food.

Cream of Celery Soup
(page 20)

GAZPACHO ANDALUZ

Metric/Imperial	American
1 small green pepper, seeded	1 small green pepper, seeded
15 cm/6 inch piece cucumber	6 inch piece cucumber
150 ml/¼ pint water	⅔ cup water
2 large cloves garlic, crushed with 1 teaspoon salt	2 large cloves garlic, crushed with 1 teaspoon salt
2 tablespoons lemon juice or cider or wine vinegar	2 tablespoons lemon juice or cider or wine vinegar
2 large slices soft white bread, broken into pieces	2 large slices soft white bread, broken into pieces
150 ml/¼ pint olive oil	⅔ cup olive oil
1 medium onion, peeled	1 medium onion, peeled
2 × 400 g/14 oz cans peeled tomatoes	2 × 14 oz cans peeled tomatoes
Tabasco sauce (optional)	Tabasco sauce (optional)

Fit the METAL BLADE and finely chop the green pepper. Place in a large bowl. Coarsely chop the cucumber and add to the pepper. Put the water, crushed garlic, lemon juice or vinegar and bread into the processor bowl and blend to a smooth purée. Slowly pour in the oil and blend again. Add to the pepper and cucumber in the bowl.

Fit the SLICING DISC and slice the onion and add to the rest of the vegetables. Press the tomatoes through a sieve to remove the seeds (pits) and add to the bowl. If consistency of soup is too thick, add a little more cold water. Chill well. Adjust seasoning and add a little Tabasco sauce if desired. Serve with bowls of chopped green pepper, cucumber and hard-boiled (cooked) eggs.

Serves 4 to 6

BROWN LENTIL SOUP

Metric/Imperial	American
450 g/1 lb brown lentils, washed and picked over	2 cups brown lentils, washed and picked over
1 litre/1¾ pints water	4¼ cups water
2 celery sticks, trimmed	2 celery sticks, trimmed
1 large carrot, scraped	1 large carrot, scraped
1 large onion, peeled and quartered	1 large onion, peeled and quartered
2 tablespoons oil	2 tablespoons oil
1.5 litres/2½ pints chicken stock	6¼ cups chicken stock
1 bay leaf	1 bay leaf
2 cloves garlic, crushed	2 cloves garlic, crushed
salt	salt
freshly ground black pepper	freshly ground black pepper

Put lentils and water in a pan and bring to the boil. Boil for 2 minutes. Remove from heat and leave to stand, covered, for 2 hours. Drain.

Fit the SLICING DISC and use to slice the celery and carrot. Set aside. Fit the METAL BLADE. Place the onion in the bowl and process until finely chopped.

Heat oil in a heavy saucepan, add the onion and brown lightly. Stir in the drained lentils, turning them well so that they become coated with oil. Add the stock and bring to the boil. Add the celery, carrot, bay leaf, garlic and salt and pepper. Simmer for 45 to 60 minutes or until the lentils are tender. Adjust seasoning.

Put half the soup in the processor bowl and purée until smooth. Return puréed soup to remainder in saucepan and reheat. If a smoother consistency is required, all the soup can be puréed.

Serves 6 to 8

CREAM OF SPINACH AND KASHA

Metric/Imperial	American
1 large onion, peeled and quartered	1 large onion, peeled and quartered
50 g/2 oz butter	$\frac{1}{4}$ cup butter
50 g/2 oz buckwheat groats	$\frac{1}{3}$ cup buckwheat groats
175 g/6 oz spinach leaves, ribs removed	6 oz spinach leaves, ribs removed
750 ml/1¼ pints good chicken stock	3 cups good chicken stock
$\frac{1}{2}$ teaspoon ground ginger	$\frac{1}{2}$ teaspoon ground ginger
$\frac{1}{2}$ teaspoon grated nutmeg	$\frac{1}{2}$ teaspoon grated nutmeg
salt	salt
freshly ground black pepper	freshly ground black pepper
150 ml/¼ pint single cream	$\frac{2}{3}$ cup light cream
fried bread croûtons, to garnish	fried bread croûtons, to garnish

Fit the METAL BLADE. Place the onion in the bowl and process until finely chopped.

Melt the butter in a pan and stir in the buckwheat and onion. Cook for a few moments then add the spinach and turn to coat in the butter. Pour in the stock and add the ginger, nutmeg, salt and pepper. Bring slowly to the boil, then cover and simmer for about 1 hour or until the buckwheat is tender.

Pour into the processor bowl and process until smooth using pulse action. Return to the rinsed pan, taste and adjust the seasoning, stir in the cream and reheat carefully. To serve, put a few croûtons into each bowl or soup cup before ladling in the soup.

Serves 6

SWEDISH TOMATO CREAM

Metric/Imperial	American
2 onions, peeled and quartered	2 onions, peeled and quartered
40 g/1½ oz butter	3 tablespoons butter
1 clove garlic, crushed	1 clove garlic, crushed
1 × 400 g/14 oz can tomatoes	1 × 14 oz can tomatoes
250 ml/8 fl oz chicken stock	1 cup chicken stock
3 teaspoons fresh dill or 1 teaspoon dried	3 teaspoons fresh dill or 1 teaspoon dried
salt	salt
freshly ground black pepper	freshly ground black pepper
3 tablespoons mayonnaise	3 tablespoons mayonnaise
few watercress leaves, to garnish	few watercress leaves, to garnish

Fit the METAL BLADE and process the onion until coarsely chopped.

Melt the butter in a saucepan, add the onion and cook gently for 5 minutes. Stir in the garlic, undrained tomatoes, stock, dill, salt and pepper. Bring to the boil and simmer for 10 minutes. Allow to cool a little then process until smooth. Blend in the mayonnaise with 2 bursts of pulse action. Pour into a bowl, cool, cover and chill. Serve in chilled soup cups garnished with watercress.

Serves 4 to 6

From left: Gazpacho Andaluz, Brown Lentil Soup and Cream of Spinach and Kasha

CREAM OF ONION SOUP

Metric/Imperial	American
50 g/2 oz Gruyère or Cheddar cheese	2 oz Gruyère or Cheddar cheese
3 onions, peeled and quartered	3 onions, peeled and quartered
40 g/1½ oz butter	3 tablespoons butter
25 g/1 oz flour	¼ cup flour
600 ml/1 pint beef stock or canned consommé	2½ cups beef stock or canned consommé
3 teaspoons meat extract	3 teaspoons meat extract
1 tablespoon Dijon mustard	1 tablespoon Dijon mustard
salt	salt
freshly ground black pepper	freshly ground black pepper
fried bread croûtons, to garnish	fried bread croûtons, to garnish

Fit the GRATING DISC and use to grate the cheese, set aside.

Fit the METAL BLADE and put the onions in the bowl. Process the onions until very finely chopped.

Melt the butter in a saucepan. Add the onions and cook slowly for 7 minutes. Sprinkle in the flour, cook for a moment or two, then pour on the stock and mix well. Bring to the boil, reduce heat and simmer for 5 minutes. Turn into the processor bowl and blend to a smooth purée. Return to the pan, stir in the meat extract, mustard, salt and pepper, then reheat gently. Pour into heated soup bowls. Garnish with the croûtons and grated cheese.

Serves 4

CREAM OF CELERY SOUP

Metric/Imperial	American
1 large head celery, including leaves	1 large head celery, including leaves
1 medium potato, peeled and cut into tube-size pieces	1 medium potato, peeled and cut into tube-size pieces
1 large onion, peeled	1 large onion, peeled
25 g/1 oz butter	2 tablespoons butter
1.2 litres/2 pints vegetable stock	5 cups vegetable stock
salt	salt
freshly ground black pepper	freshly ground black pepper
300 ml/½ pint creamy milk	1¼ cups creamy milk
TO GARNISH:	TO GARNISH:
50 g/2 oz Cheddar cheese, cut into chunks	2 oz Cheddar cheese, cut into chunks
small handful washed and dried parsley	small handful washed and dried parsley

Prepare the garnish first. Fit the GRATING DISC and grate the cheese, set aside. Fit the metal chopping blade, add the parsley and process until finely chopped. Set aside.

Place the celery, including some small leaves into the processor bowl and coarsely chop. Remove and set aside. Place the potato in the bowl and coarsely chop. Remove and set aside. Rinse the bowl, it is not necessary to wash it.

Fit the SLICING DISC and slice the onion. Melt the butter in a heavy saucepan and sauté the onion and celery until pale gold. Add the potato, stock, salt and pepper. Bring to the boil and simmer, covered, for 20 minutes.

Refit the METAL BLADE. Pour the vegetables and stock into the processor bowl, in batches, and purée. Pour back into the saucepan. Add the milk and reheat but do not allow to boil. Taste and adjust seasoning. Stir in the parsley and serve. Pass the grated cheese separately.

Serves 6

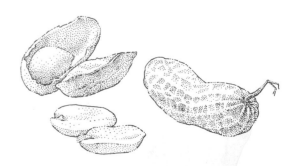

STUFFED OLIVE SOUP

Metric/Imperial	American
50 g/2 oz Gruyère or Cheddar cheese, to garnish	2 oz Gruyère or Cheddar cheese, to garnish
1 small onion, peeled and quartered	1 small onion, peeled and quartered
50 g/2 oz celery, cut into pieces	2 oz celery, cut into pieces
25 g/1 oz butter	2 tablespoons butter
750 ml/1¼ pints beef stock	3 cups beef stock
100 g/4 oz pimiento-stuffed olives, rinsed and drained	¾ cup pimiento-stuffed olives, rinsed and drained
salt	salt
freshly ground black pepper	freshly ground black pepper

Fit the GRATING DISC and use to grate the cheese. Set aside. Fit the METAL BLADE. Put the onion and celery in the processor bowl and chop using 2 or 3 bursts of pulse action.

In a saucepan, melt the butter, add the onion and celery and cook gently until softened. Stir in the stock, olives, salt and pepper. Bring to the boil, reduce heat and simmer for 15 minutes. Pour into the machine, in batches, and process until smooth. Return to pan, reheat and serve. Garnish each serving with the cheese.
Serves 4

PEANUT CREAM

Metric/Imperial	American
1 onion, peeled and quartered	1 onion, peeled and quartered
25 g/1 oz butter	2 tablespoons butter
25 g/1 oz flour	¼ cup flour
175 g/6 oz salted peanuts	1 cup salted peanuts
300 ml/½ pint chicken stock	1¼ cups chicken stock
300 ml/½ pint milk, scalded	1¼ cups milk, scalded
120 ml/4 fl oz single cream	½ cup light cream
freshly ground black pepper	freshly ground black pepper
paprika, to serve	paprika, to serve

Fit the METAL BLADE. Put onion in processor bowl and chop using 2 or 3 bursts of pulse action.

Melt the butter, add the onion and cook gently until soft. Stir in the flour and cook for 2 minutes. Stir in the peanuts and chicken stock. Bring to the boil and simmer for 15 minutes. Pour into the processor bowl, and blend until smooth. Return to the pan. Stir in the milk and cream and season with pepper. Reheat and serve very hot sprinkled with paprika.
Serves 4

CHICKEN AND BARLEY GARBURE

Metric/Imperial	American
100 g/4 oz onions, peeled	¼ lb onions, peeled
175 g/6 oz potatoes, peeled	6 oz potatoes, peeled
handful fresh parsley	handful fresh parsley
50 g/2 oz butter	¼ cup butter
40 g/1½ oz flour	6 tablespoons flour
600 ml/1 pint good chicken stock	2½ cups good chicken stock
salt	salt
freshly ground black pepper	freshly ground black pepper
50 g/2 oz pearl barley	¼ cup pearl barley
300 ml/½ pint milk, scalded	1¼ cups milk, scalded
175 g/6 oz cooked chicken, roughly chopped	6 oz cooked chicken, roughly chopped

Fit the SLICING DISC. Slice the onions and set aside. Slice the potatoes and set aside. Fit the METAL BLADE, add the parsley and process until finely chopped. Set aside.

Melt the butter and, when foaming, add the onions and cook gently until golden. Stir in the flour and cook for 2 minutes. Pour on the chicken stock, add salt and pepper and stir in the barley. Bring to the boil. Reduce heat and simmer for 20 minutes. Add the potato slices and continue cooking until the barley and potatoes are tender. Stir in the milk, chicken and parsley. Reheat and check seasoning. Serve very hot.
Serves 4

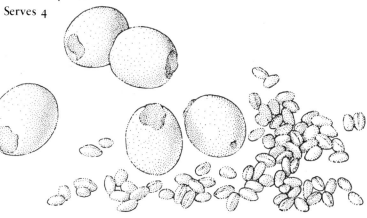

PRAWN (SHRIMP) PÂTÉ

Metric/Imperial	American
275 g/10 oz peeled prawns	1⅓ cups peeled shrimp
salt	salt
freshly ground black pepper	freshly ground black pepper
pinch ground mace	pinch ground mace
pinch cayenne pepper	pinch cayenne pepper
½ teaspoon anchovy essence	½ teaspoon anchovy extract
50 g/2 oz unsalted butter	¼ cup sweet butter
4 sprigs fresh dill or parsley, to garnish	4 sprigs fresh dill or parsley, to garnish

Fit the METAL BLADE. Put 225 g/8 oz/1¼ cups of the prawns (shrimp) into the processor bowl. Add the remaining ingredients and process until smooth. Transfer to a small saucepan, check seasoning and stir in the remaining prawns (shrimp). Bring just to the boil.

Pour into 4 individual cocottes or 1 large china dish. Smooth the top. Chill. Decorate with dill or parsley and serve with hot toast and butter.
Serves 4
Note: This pâté will keep well in the refrigerator if covered with a thin layer of clarified butter.

SMOKED MACKEREL ÉCLAIRS

Metric/Imperial	American
1 batch choux pastry (page 100)	1 batch choux paste (page 100)
smoked mackerel pâté (page 24)	smoked mackerel pâté (page 24)
mayonnaise	mayonnaise
paprika or chopped parsley	paprika or chopped parsley

Make the choux pastry in the processor, as described on page 100. Put into a piping (pastry) bag fitted with a 1 cm/½ inch plain nozzle. Grease a baking sheet and pipe finger lengths of dough onto it. Bake in a hot oven (200°C/400°F, Gas Mark 6) for 15 to 20 minutes or until golden and cooked through. Remove and cool.

Cut a slit on one side of the eclair. Pipe or spoon in the pâté. Brush the tops with mayonnaise and dust with paprika or chopped parsley.
Makes approximately 20

RAW VEGETABLE PLATTER

This is called *crudite* in France and is a large platter of freshly sliced raw vegetables. They are served with a bowl of homemade mayonnaise (see page 48), which can also be flavoured with garlic. It is an excellent dish to serve with pre-dinner drinks or as a first course. Guests help themselves to vegetables and dip them into the mayonnaise. The vegetables for serving must be crisp and fresh, preferably bought on the day you are serving them. Depending on vegetables in season, choose carrots, celery, cucumber, courgettes (zucchini), red and green peppers, chicory (endive). Leave skins on where possible and slice with slicing disc. Serve with small whole button mushrooms, spring onions (scallions), tomatoes and radishes.

MUSHROOM SALAD

Metric/Imperial	American
handful of parsley, washed and dried	handful of parsley, washed and dried
450 g/1 lb button mushrooms	4 cups button mushrooms
juice of 2 large lemons	juice of 2 large lemons
1–3 small cloves garlic crushed	1–3 small cloves garlic, crushed
salt	salt
freshly ground black pepper	freshly ground black pepper
6 tablespoons olive oil	6 tablespoons olive oil

Fit the METAL BLADE. Put the parsley in the bowl and finely chop. Remove and put in a salad bowl. Fit the SLICING DISC. Put the mushrooms in the feed tube and slice. Add to the parsley with the lemon juice, garlic, salt, pepper and oil. Toss lightly then adjust seasoning. Marinate for at least 1 hour and serve with thin, crisp dry toast.
Serves 4

From front: Mushroom Salad, Prawn Pâté and Raw Vegetable Platter

SMOKED MACKEREL PÂTÉ

Metric/Imperial	American
100 g/4 oz smoked mackerel, after skinning and boning	$\frac{1}{4}$ lb smoked mackerel, after skinning and boning
75 g/3 oz cream cheese	$\frac{1}{3}$ cup cream cheese
grated rind and juice of 1 small lemon	grated rind and juice of 1 small lemon
1 tablespoon horseradish sauce	1 tablespoon horseradish sauce
1 teaspoon prepared mustard	1 teaspoon prepared mustard
pinch of cayenne pepper	pinch of cayenne pepper
25 g/1 oz butter, softened	2 tablespoons butter, softened
salt	salt
freshly ground black pepper	freshly ground black pepper
lemon wedges, to garnish	lemon wedges, to garnish

Fit the PLASTIC BLADE. Put all the ingredients into the processor bowl, except the lemon wedges. Process for about 12 seconds or until smooth. Check seasoning. Place in a small earthenware dish. Serve chilled with lemon wedges and hot toast.
Serves 4

COARSE DUCK PÂTÉ

Metric/Imperial	American
1 small onion, peeled	1 small onion, peeled
75 g/3 oz unsalted butter	$\frac{1}{4}$ cup plus 2 tablespoons sweet butter
100 g/4 oz duck livers, trimmed	$\frac{1}{4}$ lb duck livers, trimmed
1 clove garlic, crushed	1 clove garlic, crushed
1 teaspoon fresh marjoram leaves or $\frac{1}{2}$ teaspoon dried	1 teaspoon fresh marjoram leaves or $\frac{1}{2}$ teaspoon dried
salt	salt
freshly ground black pepper	freshly ground black pepper
50 g/2 oz cooked duck, cut into pieces (optional)	$\frac{1}{4}$ cup cooked duck, cut into pieces (optional)
1 tablespoon medium sherry	1 tablespoon medium sherry
fresh bay leaf, to garnish	fresh bay leaf, to garnish

Fit the METAL BLADE and use to coarsely chop the onion.

In a small pan melt 40 g/1½ oz/3 tablespoons of the butter and sauté the livers over a brisk heat until juices appear on the surface. Reduce the heat immediately, stir in the onion, garlic, marjoram, salt and pepper and cook very gently for about 7 minutes. Add the duck pieces, if used, and cook for a further 3 minutes.

Melt the remaining butter in a small pan and tip into the processor bowl with the liver mixture and sherry. Process until coarsely chopped, about 6 to 8 seconds. Check the seasoning. Spoon into a small earthenware pot, garnish with the bay leaf and chill. Serve with hot toast and cold butter.
Serves 4

CHICKEN LIVER PÂTÉ

Metric/Imperial	American
1 small onion, peeled and quartered	1 small onion, peeled and quartered
75 g/3 oz butter	6 tablespoons butter
225 g/8 oz chicken livers, trimmed	$\frac{1}{2}$ lb chicken livers, trimmed
1 clove garlic, crushed	1 clove garlic, crushed
$\frac{1}{2}$ teaspoon grated nutmeg	$\frac{1}{2}$ teaspoon grated nutmeg
1 teaspoon fresh marjoram	1 teaspoon fresh marjoram
1 teaspoon fresh thyme	1 teaspoon fresh thyme
salt	salt
freshly ground black pepper	freshly ground black pepper
1 tablespoon brandy (optional)	1 tablespoon brandy (optional)
1 tablespoon double cream	1 tablespoon heavy cream
fresh bay leaf, to garnish	fresh bay leaf, to garnish
50 g/2 oz clarified butter, to seal	$\frac{1}{4}$ cup clarified butter, to seal

Fit the METAL BLADE and chop the onion with 2 or 3 bursts of pulse action.

In a frying pan (skillet) melt 25 g/1 oz/2 tablespoons of the butter. Add the chicken livers and cook over a brisk heat for a few minutes, then transfer the livers to the processor bowl. Stir the onion and garlic into the butter in the pan (skillet) and cook gently until soft. Tip into the processor bowl together with the nutmeg, marjoram, thyme, salt, pepper and the brandy if used. Blend until smooth. Melt the remaining butter carefully in a small pan. Allow to cool slightly and pour into the processor bowl together with the cream. Incorporate into the mixture with 2 or 3 bursts of pulse action. Adjust seasoning. Pour into a china dish. Lay the bay leaf on top. Run the clarified butter over the surface and leave to set. Serve chilled with hot toast and butter.
Serves 4

SPANISH VEGETABLE PÂTÉ

Metric/Imperial	American
1 celery stick, cut into pieces	1 celery stick, cut into pieces
½ cucumber, peeled, seeded and cut into pieces	½ cucumber, peeled, seeded and cut into pieces
½ green pepper, seeded and cut into pieces	½ green pepper, seeded and cut into pieces
1 onion, peeled and quartered	1 onion, peeled and quartered
1 × 400 g/15 oz can tomatoes	1 × 15 oz can tomatoes
2 tablespoons olive oil	2 tablespoons olive oil
1 tablespoon wine vinegar	1 tablespoon wine vinegar
1 tablespoon tomato purée	1 tablespoon tomato paste
1 clove garlic, crushed	1 clove garlic, crushed
salt	salt
freshly ground black pepper	freshly ground black pepper
pinch of cayenne pepper	pinch of cayenne pepper
1 teaspoon ground cinnamon	1 teaspoon ground cinnamon
15 g/½ oz gelatine	2 envelopes unflavored gelatin
3 tablespoons dry white wine	3 tablespoons dry white wine
½ red pepper	½ red pepper
watercress sprigs, to garnish	watercress sprigs, to garnish
mayonnaise (page 48), to serve	mayonnaise (page 48), to serve

Fit the METAL BLADE. Drop the celery, cucumber, green pepper and onion into the processor bowl and coarsely chop.

Add the tomatoes with their juice, olive oil, wine vinegar, tomato purée (paste), garlic, salt, pepper, cayenne and cinnamon. Process until the mixture forms a smooth purée (paste).

In a small bowl sprinkle the gelatine over the wine and leave to swell. Stand the bowl in hot water and stir until the gelatine has completely dissolved.

Tip the purée (paste) into a bowl, blend in the gelatine mixture and the red pepper. Taste and adjust the seasoning – a squeeze of lemon juice can be added if liked. Pour into an oiled 900 ml/1½ pint/3¾ cup mould and chill until set. Turn out, garnish with watercress and serve with mayonnaise.

Serves 4 to 6

AUBERGINE (EGGPLANT) CAVIAR

Metric/Imperial	American
1 large aubergine	1 large eggplant
1 onion, peeled and quartered	1 onion, peeled and quartered
1 clove garlic, crushed	1 clove garlic, crushed
1 large tomato, peeled and seeded	1 large tomato, peeled and seeded
1 teaspoon sugar	1 teaspoon sugar
½ teaspoon chopped fresh marjoram	½ teaspoon chopped fresh marjoram
pinch of ground allspice	pinch ground allspice
salt	salt
freshly ground black pepper	freshly ground black pepper
2 tablespoons olive oil	2 tablespoons olive oil
1 tablespoon red wine vinegar	1 tablespoon red wine vinegar

Put the whole, unpeeled aubergine (eggplant) into a large saucepan and cover with cold water. Bring to the boil, reduce heat and simmer until tender, about 20 to 30 minutes. Drain and allow to cool slightly.

Fit the METAL BLADE. Put the onion into the processor bowl with the garlic, tomato, sugar, marjoram, allspice, salt and pepper. Process until fairly finely minced (ground).

Cut the aubergine (eggplant) in half lengthways. Scoop the flesh into the bowl of onion mixture together with the oil and vinegar. Process until smooth. Check seasoning and turn into a serving dish. Smooth the top and chill well. Serve with fingers of toast, rye bread or crudités.

Serves 4

ANCHOVY TOASTS

Metric/Imperial	American
1 × 50 g/2 oz can anchovy fillets	1 × 2 oz can anchovy fillets
1 large tomato, peeled and seeded	1 large tomato, peeled and seeded
1 onion, peeled and halved	1 onion, peeled and halved
1 red pepper, seeded and quartered	1 red pepper, seeded and quartered
2 cloves garlic, crushed	2 cloves garlic, crushed
1 tablespoon red wine vinegar	1 tablespoon red wine vinegar
6 black olives, stoned	6 ripe olives, pitted
pinch chopped fresh thyme	pinch chopped fresh thyme
12 blanched almonds	12 blanched almonds
freshly ground black pepper	freshly ground black pepper
8 slices of French bread, cut diagonally	8 slices of French bread, cut diagonally
a little olive oil	a little olive oil

From left: Anchovy Toasts, Chilled Cheese Creams and Crab Fritters New Orleans served with Creole Mayonnaise (page 51)

Fit the METAL BLADE. Empty the can of anchovies, with their oil, into the processor bowl and add the tomato, onion, red pepper, garlic, vinegar, olives and thyme. Process until the onion and pepper are finely minced. Add the almonds and process until they are coarsely chopped. Season with a little black pepper.

Brush each side of the bread slices with oil and toast until crisp. Spread the anchovy mixture on each slice and grill (broil) slowly until sizzling. Serve immediately.
Serves 8

CHILLED CHEESE CREAMS

Metric/Imperial	American
50 g/2 oz Parmesan cheese	2 oz Parmesan cheese
50 g/2 oz Cheddar cheese	2 oz Cheddar cheese
50 g/2 oz Stilton cheese	2 oz Stilton cheese
1 teaspoon Dijon mustard	1 teaspoon Dijon mustard
pinch cayenne pepper	pinch cayenne pepper
salt	salt
freshly ground black pepper	freshly ground black pepper
1 teaspoon gelatine	1 teaspoon unflavored gelatin
120 ml/4 fl oz dry white wine	½ cup dry white wine
120 ml/4 fl oz double cream	½ cup heavy cream
4 stuffed olives, sliced	4 stuffed olives, sliced

Fit the GRATING DISC and use to grate the Parmesan and Cheddar cheese. Remove the cheeses and fit the PLASTIC BLADE. Place the cheeses, crumbled Stilton, mustard, cayenne, salt and pepper into the processor bowl. In a mixing bowl, sprinkle the gelatine onto the wine. Leave to swell. Stand the bowl in hot water and stir until dissolved. Pour gelatine mix into the processor bowl and blend with 2 or 3 bursts of pulse action. Lightly whisk the cream and add to the mixture. Blend again with 2 or 3 bursts of pulse action. Adjust seasoning. Pour into 4 individual cocottes and chill. Garnish with olives and serve with salted crackers.

Serves 4

Note: If you wish to turn the creams out, increase the quantity of gelatine to 2 teaspoons.

CRAB FRITTERS NEW ORLEANS

Metric/Imperial	American
100 g/4 oz flour	1 cup flour
1 teaspoon curry powder	1 teaspoon curry powder
salt	salt
freshly ground black pepper	freshly ground black pepper
200 ml/⅓ pint milk	⅞ cup milk
2 eggs	2 eggs
175 g/6 oz fresh or frozen and defrosted crabmeat, flaked	6 oz fresh or frozen and defrosted crabmeat, flaked
50 g/2 oz cold boiled rice	⅓ cup cold boiled rice
oil for shallow frying	oil for shallow frying
TO GARNISH AND SERVE:	TO GARNISH AND SERVE:
few unshelled prawns	few unshelled shrimps
parsley sprigs	parsley sprigs
Creole mayonnaise (page 51)	Creole mayonnaise (page 51)

Fit the PLASTIC BLADE. Place the flour, curry powder, salt and pepper in the bowl and combine with 2 bursts of pulse action. Add the milk and eggs, and process until smooth. Pour in a bowl and leave for 30 minutes. Stir the crab and rice into the batter.

Pour cooking oil to a depth of 1 cm/½ inch in a frying pan (skillet) and heat slowly. Slide tablespoons of the mixture into the hot oil and cook until golden on each side. Drain on kitchen paper and arrange on a hot serving dish. Garnish with the prawns (shrimp) and parsley and serve with Creole mayonnaise.

Serves 4

CUCUMBER MOUSSE

Metric/Imperial	American
15 cm/6 inch piece cucumber	6 inch piece cucumber
2 teaspoons tarragon or cider vinegar	2 teaspoons tarragon or cider vinegar
¼ teaspoon dried tarragon	¼ teaspoon dried tarragon
275 g/10 oz curd or cream cheese	1¼ cups curd or cream cheese
2½ teaspoons gelatine	2½ teaspoons unflavored gelatin
150 ml/¼ pint good chicken stock	⅔ cup good chicken stock
TO GARNISH:	TO GARNISH:
7 cm/3 inch piece cucumber	3 inch piece cucumber
5 tablespoons chicken stock	⅓ cup chicken stock
½ teaspoon gelatine	½ teaspoon unflavored gelatin

Fit the METAL BLADE. Place the 15 cm/6 inch piece cucumber, the vinegar, tarragon and cheese in the processor bowl and blend until smooth. Dissolve the gelatine in 2 tablespoons of the stock. Cool quickly and pour through the feed tube with the remaining stock. Blend using pulse action in two or three bursts. Divide between six individual ramekins and chill until set. Once set, prepare the garnish.

Fit the SLICING DISC and use to slice the cucumber. Dissolve the gelatine in the stock and cool slightly. Pour a thin layer of gelatine mixture over each dish and garnish with cucumber slices. Chill for a further 30 minutes. Serve with Melba toast.

Serves 6

BAGNA CAUDA WITH HOT CHEESE AND ANCHOVY DIP

Metric/Imperial	American
100 g/4 oz Cheddar cheese	¼ lb Cheddar cheese
1 small onion, peeled and quartered	1 small onion, peeled and quartered
1 large tomato, peeled and seeded	1 large tomato, peeled and seeded
15 g/½ oz butter	1 tablespoon butter
1 teaspoon flour	1 teaspoon flour
1 tablespoon anchovy essence	1 tablespoon anchovy extract
few drops Tabasco sauce	few drops Tabasco sauce
salt	salt
freshly ground black pepper	freshly ground black pepper

Fit the GRATING DISC and use to grate the cheese, set aside. Fit the METAL BLADE.

Put the onion into the processor bowl and process until coarsely chopped. Add the tomato and continue processing until finely minced (ground).

Melt the butter in a pan and add the onion and tomato. Cook until soft then stir in the flour. Cook for a further 2 minutes, then add the remaining ingredients and the cheese, mix well. Adjust seasoning. Simmer gently for 5 minutes. Pour into a heated dish and serve hot with the following chilled, prepared vegetables: whole radishes; quartered, canned artichoke hearts; spring onions (scallions); cherry tomatoes; cauliflower florets; deep-fried matchstick potatoes and potato or corn crisps (chips). Use the SLICING DISC to prepare the following: green and red peppers; carrots; cucumber; deep fried onion rings and courgettes (zucchini).

SHERRY SPREAD

Metric/Imperial	American
25 g/1 oz walnuts	¼ cup walnuts
225 g/8 oz cream or curd cheese	1 cup cream or curd cheese
2 tablespoons medium or dry sherry	2 tablespoons medium or dry sherry
8 black olives, stoned and chopped	8 ripe olives, pitted and chopped
mild curry paste, to taste	mild curry paste, to taste

Fit the METAL BLADE. Finely chop the walnuts and add all other ingredients. Blend to a smooth paste using pulse action. Chill well. Serve with crackers.

Makes 225 g/8 oz/1 cup

FOUNDATION SPREAD

Metric/Imperial	American
50 g/2 oz blanched almonds	½ cup blanched almonds
225 g/8 oz soft margarine	1 cup soft margarine
2 tablespoons boiling water	2 tablespoons boiling water

Fit the METAL BLADE and finely chop the almonds. Add the margarine and blend with pulse action. Pour in the boiling water and blend.

To this foundation, add your choice of: 2 tablespoons mild curry paste or 100 g/4 oz (1 cup) grated Cheddar cheese with 2 teaspoons lemon juice or 100 g/4 oz (1 cup) coarsely chopped mushrooms with 1 tablespoon sherry. Season all to taste with salt and pepper.

Serve with crackers and other dips or use as a spread for bread.

Makes 225 g/8 oz/1 cup

STILTON AND WALNUT SPREAD

Metric/Imperial	American
100 g/4 oz walnuts	1 cup walnuts
225 g/8 oz Stilton cheese, cut into pieces	½ lb Stilton cheese, cut into pieces
50 g/2 oz butter, softened	¼ cup butter, softened
3 tablespoons port	3 tablespoons port

Fit the METAL BLADE. Place the walnuts in the bowl and process until coarsely chopped. Reserve. Put the cheese, butter and port into the bowl and process until smooth. Add the walnuts using 3 bursts of pulse action. Pack the spread into small earthenware pots, cover and chill.

This spread keeps for at least 3 weeks in the refrigerator.

Makes 350 g/12 oz/¾ lb

SALADS AND VEGETABLES

An old Spanish proverb says 'For a salad you need four people, a spendthrift for oil, a miser for vinegar, a counsellor for salt and a madman to stir it all up'.

Today you can do without the madman and use your processor instead. Use the processor to emulsify dressings, combine ingredients and to chop, slice, grate or purée vegetables. Because of the speed of the machine, salads for a cold meal can be made up at the last moment so they are served at their best.

Try imaginative combinations of salad ingredients to bring out subtle flavours. Bean Sprout Slaw, American Beetroot (Beet) and Cabbage salad, Fennel and Lemon Salad or Spinach and Walnut Salad are just some ideas.

For people following a low-cholesterol diet, vegetable and salad dishes make up a large part of the diet, while for vegetarians, they play an important part in providing nutritious meals.

With a food processor, potato dishes seem easier and quicker. The slicing for Gratin Dauphinois or Potatoes Anna is done in seconds, with slices of potato the same thickness that cook evenly. Any of the recipes that are garnished can have the garnish prepared ahead and stored; see the chapter on Short Cut Ingredients (page 119).

Presentation is important for all foods and an attractively arranged or garnished dish will tempt the most fussy eater. Some children are loath to eat salads or vegetables, so serve usual vegetables prepared in new ways in the food processor – either finely chopped, sliced, grated or puréed.

Spinach and Walnut Salad (page 33)

AMERICAN BEETROOT (BEET) SALAD

Metric/Imperial	American
½ small red cabbage, rinsed and trimmed into tube-size pieces	½ small red cabbage, rinsed and trimmed into tube-size pieces
225 g/8 oz pickled beetroot, drained and roughly chopped	1⅓ cups roughly chopped pickled beets
1 onion, peeled and quartered	1 onion, peeled and quartered
1 tablespoon prepared horseradish sauce	1 tablespoon prepared horseradish sauce
2 tablespoons lemon juice	2 tablespoons lemon juice
1 tablespoon golden syrup	1 tablespoon maple syrup
1 clove garlic, crushed	1 clove garlic, crushed
2 tablespoons mayonnaise	2 tablespoons mayonnaise
1 teaspoon Dijon mustard	1 teaspoon Dijon mustard
salt	salt
freshly ground black pepper	freshly ground black pepper
celery curls, to garnish	celery curls, to garnish

Fit the GRATING DISC. Feed the cabbage into the feed tube and shred. Remove and place in a large bowl. Process the beetroot (beet) and onion in the same way and add to the cabbage. Mix the remaining ingredients, except the celery, together. Pour over vegetables and toss well. Adjust seasoning. Cover and chill.

Serve in a wooden salad bowl, garnished with the celery.
Serves 4

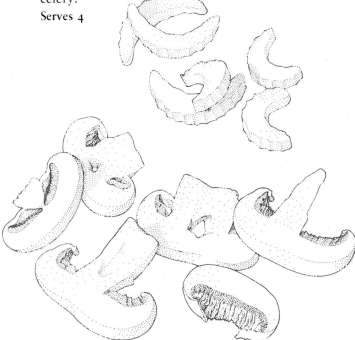

CHILDREN'S SALAD

Metric/Imperial	American
50 g/2 oz Cheddar cheese	2 oz Cheddar cheese
1 medium carrot, scraped	1 medium carrot, scraped
225 g/8 oz white cabbage	·½ lb white cabbage
1 dessert apple	1 dessert apple
50 g/2 oz sultanas	⅓ cup seedless white raisins
1 teaspoon brown sugar	1 teaspoon brown sugar
1 tablespoon lemon juice	1 tablespoon lemon juice
homemade salad cream (page 53)	homemade salad cream (page 53)
TO GARNISH:	TO GARNISH:
5 cm/2 inch piece carrot	2 inch piece carrot

Fit the GRATING DISC. Place the cheese in the feed tube and grate. Put in a salad bowl. Grate the carrot and put into the bowl. Fit the SLICING DISC. Shred the cabbage and add to the carrot. Fit the METAL BLADE. Using pulse action, chop the apple and add to the bowl. Add the sultanas (raisins), sugar, lemon juice and a little salad cream to the salad bowl and toss lightly to mix. Cut the carrot into ribbons, using a swivel-bladed peeler and use to garnish the salad.
Serves 4

CHEF'S SALAD

Metric/Imperial	American
100 g/4 oz mushrooms	1 cup mushrooms
2 sticks celery, trimmed	2 sticks celery, trimmed
175–250 g/6–8 oz lean cold roast pork, rare roast beef or cooked ham	6–8 oz lean cold roast pork, rare roast beef or cooked ham
100 g/4 oz fresh spinach, well washed and torn into pieces	¼ lb fresh spinach, well washed and torn into pieces
1 soft lettuce, torn into pieces	1 soft lettuce, torn into pieces
2 hard-boiled eggs, quartered	2 hard-cooked eggs, quartered
herb flavoured vinaigrette	herb flavored vinaigrette
75 g/3 oz Gruyère cheese	3 oz Gruyère cheese

Fit the SLICING DISC. Slice the mushrooms, celery and meat separately and put into a salad bowl. Add the spinach, lettuce pieces and eggs to the salad bowl. Toss together lightly with the vinaigrette. Slice the cheese and scatter over the salad.
Serves 4 to 6

SPINACH AND WALNUT SALAD

Metric/Imperial	American
25 g/1 oz walnuts	$\frac{1}{4}$ cup walnuts
3 shallots or 1 small onion, peeled	3 shallots or 1 small onion, peeled
75 g/3 oz young spinach leaves, washed, ribs removed and shaken dry	$\frac{1}{2}$ cup young spinach leaves, washed, ribs removed and shaken dry
2 teaspoons white wine vinegar	2 teaspoons white wine vinegar
2 tablespoons walnut or olive oil	2 tablespoons walnut oil or olive oil
salt	salt
freshly ground black pepper	freshly ground black pepper

Fit the METAL BLADE. Place the walnuts in the bowl and coarsely chop using 3 bursts of pulse action. Reserve. Put shallots or onion into bowl and process until finely minced (ground). Reserve.

Tear the spinach leaves into pieces and put into a wooden salad bowl. Stir in the walnuts and shallots or onion. Cover and chill.

Pour vinegar and oil into the processor bowl with a little salt and pepper, and blend with 3 bursts of pulse action. Adjust seasoning. When ready to serve, pour the dressing over the salad and toss well to coat the leaves. Serve immediately.

Serves 4

CUCUMBER JELLIED SALAD

Metric/Imperial	American
2 large cucumbers, peeled	2 large cucumbers, peeled
120 ml/4 fl oz cold water	$\frac{1}{2}$ cup cold water
15 g/$\frac{1}{2}$ oz gelatine, soaked in 3 tablespoons cold water	2 envelopes unflavored gelatin, soaked in 3 tablespoons cold water
2 teaspoons finely chopped onion	2 teaspoons finely chopped onion
1 tablespoon dill-flavoured or white wine vinegar	1 tablespoon dill-flavored or white wine vinegar
salt	salt
freshly ground black pepper	freshly ground black pepper
pinch cayenne pepper	pinch cayenne pepper
green colouring	green coloring
225 g/8 oz white or black grapes, pipped	2 cups white or purple grapes, pitted
4 tablespoons mayonnaise	4 tablespoons mayonnaise

Fit the SLICING DISC and use to slice the cucumbers. Reserve 12 of the best slices and put remainder in a pan with cold water. Cook gently until soft.

Fit the METAL BLADE. Pour the cucumber and liquid into the processor bowl and process until smooth. Pour the mixture into a bowl and stir in the gelatine which has been dissolved over hot water. Add the onion, vinegar, salt, pepper and cayenne, and sufficient colouring to make the liquid pale green. Pour into a wetted 900 ml/1$\frac{1}{2}$ pint/3$\frac{3}{4}$ cup ring mould and chill until set.

Turn the mould onto a chilled serving dish. Mix the grapes and mayonnaise lightly together and fill the centre of the ring. Garnish with the remaining cucumber slices around the edge.

Serves 6

SLIMMERS' LUNCH IN A GLASS

*From left: Fennel and Lemon Salad,
Slimmers' Lunch in a Glass
and Mykonos Salad*

Metric/Imperial	American
300 ml/½ pint carrot juice, freshly made or canned	1¼ cups carrot juice, freshly made or canned
300 ml/½ pint tomato juice	1¼ cups tomato juice
300 ml/½ pint natural yogurt	1¼ cups unflavored yogurt
lemon slices	lemon slices
salt or garlic salt (optional)	salt or garlic salt (optional)

Fit the PLASTIC BLADE. Using pulse action, blend the
carrot juice, tomato juice and yogurt in bursts.
Remove and chill. Serve in tall glasses, with a lemon
slice in each one, and salt if liked.

Makes 900 ml/1½ pints /3¾ cups

FENNEL AND LEMON SALAD

Metric/Imperial	American
1 large fennel bulb	1 large fennel bulb
handful of parsley, washed and well dried	handful of parsley, washed and well dried
1 tablespoon lemon juice	1 tablespoon lemon juice
2 tablespoons olive or groundnut oil	2 tablespoons olive or peanut oil
1 teaspoon sugar (optional)	1 teaspoon sugar (optional)
2 tablespoons double cream	2 tablespoons heavy cream
salt	salt
freshly ground black pepper	freshly ground black pepper
1 lemon	1 lemon

Wash the fennel, if necessary, then cut into thin slices about 7 cm/3 inch long. Fit the SLICING DISC. Press the fennel pieces through the feed tube with the pusher to make julienne strips. Fit the METAL BLADE and finely chop the parsley. Remove and set aside. Pour in lemon juice, oil, sugar if used, cream, salt, and pepper and blend, using pulse action.

Soak the fennel in very cold water for a few minutes, then drain and dry. Peel rind from lemon, cut away pith. Slice lemon into thin slices and cut each slice into quarters.

Combine fennel, lemon and parsley and toss in the dressing. Serve with roast pork or veal.

Serves 4

MYKONOS SALAD

Metric/Imperial	American
1 lemon	1 lemon
15 cm/6 inch piece cucumber	6 inch piece cucumber
1 small red pepper, seeded	1 small red pepper, seeded
1 small green pepper, seeded	1 small green pepper, seeded
1 medium onion, peeled and quartered	1 medium onion, peeled and quartered
1 clove garlic, crushed	1 clove garlic, crushed
freshly ground black pepper	freshly ground black pepper
2 tablespoons olive oil	2 tablespoons olive oil
salt	salt
100 g/4 oz black olives	3/4 cup ripe olives
2 hard-boiled eggs, quartered	2 hard-cooked eggs, quartered
4 small tomatoes, peeled and quartered	4 small tomatoes, peeled and quartered
Cos lettuce, to serve	lettuce, to serve

Grate the lemon, set the rind aside and reserve the whole lemon. Fit the SLICING DISC.

Slice the cucumber, peppers and onions separately and put into a salad bowl. Fit the METAL BLADE.

Remove the pith from the lemon, cut into quarters then coarsely chop using pulse action.

In a screw top jar combine the lemon, garlic, pepper, and oil and shake well to make a dressing. Add salt if necessary.

Add olives, eggs and tomatoes to the salad bowl. Lightly toss in the dressing and scatter the lemon rind on top. Serve on a bed of lettuce.

Serves 4

ORANGE BEETROOT (BEET) SALAD

Metric/Imperial	American
3 small, cooked beetroot, peeled	3 small, cooked beets, peeled
3 small onions, peeled	3 small onions, peeled
juice of 1 orange	juice of 1 orange
1 orange	1 orange
2–3 tablespoons vinaigrette	2–3 tablespoons vinaigrette
small bunch watercress, rinsed and trimmed	small bunch watercress, rinsed and trimmed

Fit the SLICING DISC. Slice the beetroot and onions and put into a bowl. Mix together then pour over the orange juice and leave for 30 minutes.

Cut all the peel and pith from the orange then cut between the membrane and separate the segments, reserve. Pour the dressing over the onion mixture and toss. Turn into a chilled salad bowl or glass dish. Put the watercress into the centre of the dish and arrange orange segments around the edge at intervals.

A good salad to serve with cold poultry and game.
Serves 2

BEAN SPROUT SLAW

Metric/Imperial	American
350 g/12 oz tight white cabbage, washed, cored and cut into tube-size pieces	¾ lb tight white cabbage, washed, cored and cut into tube-size pieces
1 red pepper, cored, seeded and cut in half	1 red pepper, cored, seeded and cut in half
100 g/4 oz bean sprouts	2 cups bean sprouts
3 tablespoons mayonnaise (page 48)	3 tablespoons mayonnaise (page 48)
50 g/2 oz blue cheese	2 oz blue cheese
1 tablespoon lemon juice	1 tablespoon lemon juice
salt	salt
freshly ground black pepper	freshly ground black pepper

Fit the SLICING DISC. Put cabbage into the feed tube and slice. Put the red pepper in the feed tube and slice. Place the cabbage and pepper into a large bowl and chill the bean sprouts. Toss well together. Cover and chill.

While the salad is chilling, make the dressing. Fit the PLASTIC BLADE. Put the mayonnaise, cheese, lemon

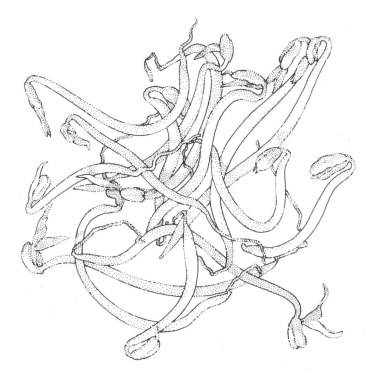

GERMAN POTATO SALAD

Metric/Imperial	American
4 medium, waxy potatoes, peeled	4 medium, waxy potatoes, peeled
2 sticks celery, washed and trimmed	2 sticks celery, washed and trimmed
6 spring onions or 1 medium onion, peeled	6 scallions or 1 medium onion, peeled
3 tablespoons cider vinegar	3 tablespoons cider vinegar
1 tablespoon dill seeds	1 tablespoon dill seeds
salt	salt
freshly ground black pepper	freshly ground black pepper
½ teaspoon dry mustard	½ teaspoon dry mustard
homemade mayonnaise (page 48)	homemade mayonnaise (page 48)
TO GARNISH:	TO GARNISH:
½ green pepper, seeded	½ green pepper, seeded

Cook the potatoes until tender but not overcooked. Drain well and allow to cool. Fit the SLICING DISC. Slice the potatoes and place in a salad bowl.

Slice the celery and onions and add to the potatoes. Mix the vinegar, dill, salt, pepper, mustard and mayonnaise and lightly stir through the potato mixture with a wooden spoon, taking care not to overmix. Chill. Serve garnished with sliced green pepper (use slicing disc) scattered over.
Serves 6

juice, salt and pepper into the bowl, and process until smooth. Set aside.

Pour the dressing over the slaw and toss well. Serve chilled.
Serves 4

MARINATED VEGETABLE SALAD

Metric/Imperial	American
50 g/2 oz blanched almonds	½ cup blanched almonds
½ red pepper, seeded	½ red pepper, seeded
½ green pepper, seeded	½ green pepper, seeded
100 g/4 oz cauliflower florets	¼ lb cauliflower florets
1 tablespoon wine vinegar	1 tablespoon wine vinegar
½ teaspoon dried tarragon	½ teaspoon dried tarragon
salt	salt
freshly ground black pepper	freshly ground black pepper
4 tablespoons vegetable or olive oil	¼ cup vegetable or olive oil
100 g/4 oz firm button mushrooms, cleaned	1 cup firm button mushrooms, cleaned
small bunch of watercress, washed and trimmed into sprigs	small bunch of watercress, washed and trimmed into sprigs

Fit the GRATING DISC and use to shred the almonds. Put into a large bowl. Fit the SLICING DISC and use to slice the peppers. Add to the bowl with the cauliflower. Fit the PLASTIC BLADE. Put the vinegar, tarragon, salt, pepper and oil into the bowl. Process using pulse action until combined. Adjust seasoning. Pour over the vegetables and leave to marinate overnight.

Fit the SLICING DISC and use to slice the mushrooms. Add the mushrooms and watercress to the salad and toss lightly. Serve chilled.
Serves 4

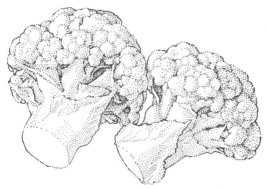

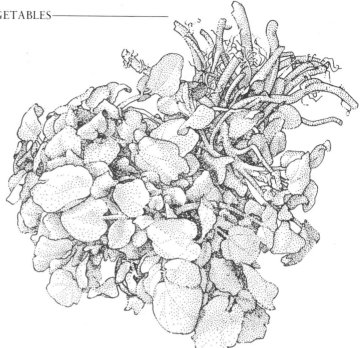

PRAWN (SHRIMP) SALAD

Metric/Imperial	American
1 medium head of celery	1 medium head of celery
50 g/2 oz walnut pieces	⅓ cup walnut pieces
4 red skinned eating apples	4 red skinned eating apples
3 tablespoons special herb vinaigrette (page 53)	3 tablespoons special herb vinaigrette (page 53)
4–5 tablespoons mayonnaise (page 48)	4–5 tablespoons mayonnaise (page 48)
225 g/8 oz shelled prawns	1¼ cups shelled shrimp
TO GARNISH:	TO GARNISH:
lettuce leaves	lettuce leaves
1 small avocado or parsley	1 small avocado or parsley

Fit the SLICING DISC. Cut the celery into tube length pieces and put into the feed tube. Slice the celery and put into a bowl.

Fit the METAL BLADE and use to roughly chop the walnuts. Remove and set aside. Core the apples then cut into large pieces. Process the apples, using pulse action, until diced, then add to the celery. Combine the vinaigrette and mayonnaise and fold into the celery and apple with the prawns (shrimp). Add a little more mayonnaise if necessary. Chill for 30 minutes. When ready to serve stir through the walnuts.

Line individual dishes or one salad bowl with lettuce leaves. Spoon in the salad and garnish with the sliced avocado or chopped parsley, prepared in the processor.
Serves 4 to 6

ORANGE GLAZED CARROTS

Metric/Imperial	American
handful of parsley, washed and well dried	handful of parsley, washed and well dried
6 medium carrots, scraped and cut into tube-size pieces	6 medium carrots, scraped and cut into tube-size pieces
3 tablespoons orange juice	3 tablespoons orange juice
$1\frac{1}{2}$ tablespoons soft brown sugar	$1\frac{1}{2}$ tablespoons light brown sugar
50 g/2 oz butter or margarine	$\frac{1}{4}$ cup butter or margarine
6 cloves	6 cloves
salt	salt
freshly ground black pepper	freshly ground black pepper

Fit the METAL BLADE. Chop the parsley as fine or as coarse as you wish. Set aside.

Fit the SLICING DISC. Feed the carrots into the tube. Pack tightly and press down firmly with pusher for even slices. Cook the carrot slices in a small quantity of boiling salted water until just tender but still crisp. Drain and place in a serving dish, keep warm.

Put the orange juice, sugar, butter or margarine, cloves, salt and pepper into a saucepan and heat to simmering point. Remove the cloves with a slotted spoon and pour the sauce over the carrots. Leave for a few minutes before serving sprinkled with the parsley.

Serves 4

BURGUNDIAN CABBAGE

Metric/Imperial	American
2 onions, peeled and halved	2 onions, peeled and halved
$\frac{1}{2}$ small red cabbage, rinsed and trimmed	$\frac{1}{2}$ small red cabbage, rinsed and trimmed
50 g/2 oz butter	$\frac{1}{4}$ cup butter
300 ml/$\frac{1}{2}$ pint dry red wine	$1\frac{1}{4}$ cups dry red wine
300 ml/$\frac{1}{2}$ pint good beef stock	$1\frac{1}{4}$ cups good beef stock
salt	salt
freshly ground black pepper	freshly ground black pepper
pinch of ground cloves	pinch of ground cloves
grated rind of 1 orange	grated rind of 1 orange
40 g/$1\frac{1}{2}$ oz plain flour	$\frac{1}{4}$ cup plus 2 tablespoons all-purpose flour
chopped parsley, to garnish	chopped parsley, to garnish

GRATIN DAUPHINOIS

Metric/Imperial	American
450 g/1 lb potatoes, peeled	1 lb potatoes, peeled
salt	salt
freshly ground black pepper	freshly ground black pepper
grated nutmeg	grated nutmeg
150 ml/$\frac{1}{4}$ pint double cream	$\frac{2}{3}$ cup heavy cream
300 ml/$\frac{1}{2}$ pint milk, or enough to cover the potatoes	1$\frac{1}{4}$ cups milk, or enough to cover the potatoes
25 g/1 oz butter	2 tablespoons butter
chopped parsley (optional)	chopped parsley (optional)

Fit the SLICING DISC and use to slice the onions, then the cabbage.

In a large pan, melt the butter, stir in the onions and cabbage and turn them over thoroughly in the fat. Cook for 5 minutes. Stir in the wine, stock, salt, pepper, cloves and orange rind. Bring to the boil, reduce heat, cover and simmer for at least 1 hour. The cabbage should be very soft. Strain off the liquid into a jug and reserve.

In a small bowl, mix the flour with a little of the reserved cooking liquid. Stir until smooth. Add remaining liquid and put into a small pan. Bring to the boil, stirring all the time and cook gently for 5 minutes. Adjust the seasoning then pour over the cabbage and reheat carefully. Place in a heated serving dish and sprinkle with parsley, chopped in the processor. Serve with pork sausages.

Serves 4

Fit the SLICING DISC. Cut the potatoes into tube-size pieces and push through the slicer. Rinse in cold water and pat dry.

Butter a gratin dish and arrange the potatoes in layers, seasoning each layer with salt, pepper and nutmeg. Stir half the cream into the milk and pour over the potato slices. Dot the butter over the top and bake in a moderate oven (180°C/350°F, Gas Mark 4) for 1$\frac{3}{4}$ hours. Pour the remaining cream over and return to the oven for a further 20 minutes, or until the liquid is reduced and the potatoes are golden brown. Sprinkle with the parsley, which has been chopped in the processor.

Serves 4

POTATOES ANNA

This is normally a time consuming recipe to prepare. A food processor does the work in seconds.

Metric/Imperial	American
750 g/1½ lb potatoes, peeled and cut into tube-size pieces	1½ lb potatoes, peeled and cut into tube-size pieces
salt	salt
freshly ground black pepper	freshly ground black pepper
100 g/4 oz butter or margarine, melted	½ cup butter or margarine, melted

Fit the SLICING DISC. Generously butter a round, shallow ovenproof dish. Press the potatoes firmly down into tube with the pusher and slice. Make concentric circles of the potato in the dish, overlapping the slices slightly. Season each layer with salt and pepper and sprinkle with the melted butter. Continue until all potatoes have been used, pressing each layer down slightly. Cover with foil and bake in a moderately hot oven (190°C/ 375°F, Gas Mark 5) for 30 minutes. Remove the foil and bake for a further 30 minutes.

Serves 4 to 6

PARSNIPS AND POTATO SCALLOP

Metric/Imperial	American
2 slices fresh bread, crusts removed	2 slices fresh bread, crusts removed
75 g/3 oz mature Cheddar cheese	3 oz mature Cheddar cheese
225 g/8 oz parsnips, peeled	½ lb parsnips, peeled
225 g/8 oz potatoes, peeled	½ lb potatoes, peeled
100 g/4 oz firm button mushrooms, cleaned	1 cup firm button mushrooms, cleaned
300 ml/½ pint béchamel sauce	1¼ cups béchamel sauce
2 teaspoons grated nutmeg	2 teaspoons grated nutmeg
Dijon mustard	Dijon mustard
salt	salt
freshly ground black pepper	freshly ground black pepper
TO GARNISH AND SERVE:	TO GARNISH AND SERVE:
grilled bacon rolls	broiled bacon rolls
chopped parsley	chopped parsley
whole baked tomatoes, rubbed with garlic	whole baked tomatoes, rubbed with garlic

Fit the METAL BLADE. Place bread in processor bowl and process to fine crumbs, set aside. Fit the GRATING DISC. Grate the cheese and set aside. Fit the SLICING DISC and slice the parsnips, potatoes and mushrooms. Put into a large bowl and toss well together.

Heat the béchamel sauce and stir in the nutmeg, mustard, salt and pepper. Generously butter an oval gratin dish and put in the vegetables. Pour the sauce over then tap the dish once or twice on a hard surface to settle the sauce. Mix together the breadcrumbs and cheese and sprinkle evenly over the top. Bake in a moderate oven (180°C/350°F, Gas Mark 4) for about 1 hour or until the vegetables are tender and the top is golden. Garnish with the bacon rolls and parsley, chopped in the processor. Serve with whole baked tomatoes rubbed with garlic.

Serves 4

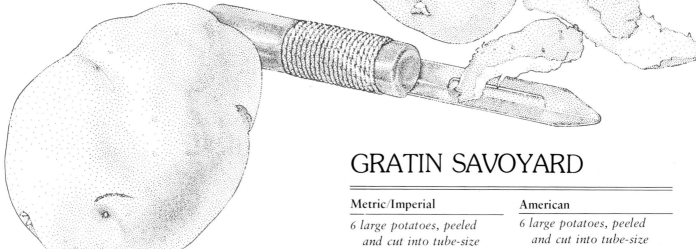

GRATIN SAVOYARD

Metric/Imperial	American
6 large potatoes, peeled and cut into tube-size pieces	6 large potatoes, peeled and cut into tube-size pieces
1 large knob celeriac, peeled and cut into tube-size pieces	1 large knob celeriac, peeled and cut into tube-size pieces
100 g/4 oz Gruyère or Edam cheese	¼ lb Gruyère or Edam cheese
butter for greasing	butter for greasing
salt	salt
freshly ground black pepper	freshly ground black pepper
150 ml/¼ pint chicken stock	⅔ cup chicken stock

Fit the SLICING DISC. Place the potato into the feed tube. Press down with pusher and slice. Remove and place in a bowl of cold salted water. Slice celeriac in the same way, remove and set aside. Rinse the bowl and dry well.

Fit the GRATING DISC and use to grate the cheese.

Generously butter a baking dish and make alternate layers of celeriac, drained potatoes and cheese, reserving 3 tablespoons of the cheese and ending with a layer of potatoes. Sprinkle with salt and pepper as you go. Bring the stock to a boil and pour over the vegetables. Bake in a moderately hot oven (190°C/375°F, Gas Mark 5) for 1 to 1¼ hours, or until the potatoes are tender and most of the liquid has been absorbed. Sprinkle with the remaining cheese and return to the oven until brown and bubbling.

Serves 6 to 8

POTATO CRISPS (CHIPS)

You'll never want to buy a packet again, as these are almost as much fun to make as they are to eat.

Metric/Imperial	American
good firm potatoes, peeled and cut into tube-size pieces	good firm potatoes, peeled and cut into tube-size pieces
oil for deep-frying	oil for deep fat-frying
salt, onion salt or garlic salt	salt, onion salt or garlic salt

Fit the SLICING DISC. Put the potatoes into the feed tube and slice. Soak the slices in cold water for 30 minutes. This removes some starch and ensures that the slices brown evenly. Dry well in a clean tea-towel then chill in the refrigerator.

Heat oil in a deep-frying pan to 182°C/360°F. Fry the potatoes, in batches, for 2 to 3 minutes or until tender but not brown. Drain well. Heat oil to 190°C/375°F and fry crisps (chips) only until crisp and golden. Drain well on kitchen paper and toss with salt.

RÖSTI

Metric/Imperial	American
450 g/1 lb potatoes, scrubbed	1 lb potatoes, scrubbed
salt	salt
100 g/4 oz shallots or onions, peeled	¼ lb shallots or onions, peeled
freshly ground black pepper	freshly ground black pepper
50 g/2 oz unsalted butter	¼ cup sweet butter

Cook the potatoes in boiling salted water until just tender. Drain well and chill. This is most important. Peel the potatoes and cut into pieces to fit the feed tube. Fit the GRATING DISC. Put the potatoes in the tube and grate. Set aside.

Fit the METAL BLADE. Put the shallots or onions into the bowl and process until finely chopped. Gently mix the onion into the potatoes adding salt and pepper to taste.

Melt 25 g/1 oz/2 tablespoons of the butter in an 18 cm/7 inch frying pan (skillet). Add the potato mixture and flatten with a palette knife. Cook over a gentle heat until golden brown and crisp underneath. Slide onto a plate and invert onto another plate.

Melt the remaining butter in the pan (skillet), slide the uncooked side into it and cook until the bottom is golden and crisp. Turn onto a heated serving dish and cut into wedges. Serve with roasted or grilled (broiled) meats.

Serves 4

SPINACH GRATIN

Metric/Imperial	American
2 slices dry bread, trimmed and broken into pieces	2 slices dry bread, trimmed and broken into pieces
50 g/2 oz Gruyère cheese, cut up roughly	2 oz Gruyère cheese, cut up roughly
450 g/1 lb spinach, cooked and drained or 350 g/12 oz frozen spinach, cooked and drained	1 lb spinach, cooked and drained or 12 oz frozen spinach, cooked and drained
½ teaspoon grated nutmeg	½ teaspoon grated nutmeg
salt	salt
freshly ground black pepper	freshly ground black pepper
25 g/1 oz butter or margarine, melted	2 tablespoons butter or margarine, melted

Fit the METAL BLADE. Drop the bread through the feed tube and process to coarse breadcrumbs. Remove and set aside. Fit the GRATING DISC and use to grate the cheese.

Mix the spinach with the nutmeg, salt, pepper and half the cheese. Place in a buttered shallow ovenproof dish. Mix the remaining cheese with the breadcrumbs and sprinkle over the top. Pour the melted butter or margarine over. Bake in a hot oven (230°C/450°F, Gas Mark 8) for about 15 minutes, until brown.
Serves 4 to 6

WINTER WARMER

Metric/Imperial	American
750 g/1½ lb potatoes, peeled	1½ lb potatoes, peeled
450 g/1 lb onions, peeled	1 lb onions, peeled
600 ml/1 pint thick hot white sauce	2½ cups thick hot white sauce
salt	salt
freshly ground black pepper	freshly ground black pepper
½ teaspoon dried basil	½ teaspoon dried basil
½ teaspoon dried marjoram	½ teaspoon dried marjoram
225–350 g/8–12 oz cooked ham, gammon or boiled bacon, cut into tube-size pieces	8–12 oz cooked or boiled ham, cut into tube-size pieces

*Left, from rear: Rösti,
Spinach Gratin and
Nutty Baked Onions*

Fit the SLICING DISC. Slice the potatoes and onions. Season the white sauce well with salt, pepper, basil and marjoram. Put meat into feed tube, press down firmly with pusher, and slice.

In a greased casserole, make layers of the potatoes and onions, laying the meat slices between. Season the layers. Pour over the hot sauce. Cover and bake in a moderate oven (180°C/350°F, Gas Mark 4) for 1 hour. Uncover, and bake for a further 30 minutes or until top is well browned. Serve with a green vegetable or tossed salad and garlic bread.
Serves 4

NUTTY BAKED ONIONS

Metric/Imperial	American
175 g/6 oz salted peanuts	¾ cup salted peanuts
350 g/12 oz onions, peeled	¾ lb onions, peeled
300 ml/½ pint milk	1¼ cups milk
1 bay leaf	1 bay leaf
25 g/1 oz butter	2 tablespoons butter
25 g/1 oz flour	¼ cup flour
salt	salt
freshly ground black pepper	freshly ground black pepper
pinch grated nutmeg	pinch grated nutmeg
TO GARNISH (optional):	TO GARNISH (optional):
grilled tomato halves	broiled tomato halves
parsley	parsley

Fit the METAL BLADE. Put the peanuts in the bowl and process until fairly finely ground. Set aside. Fit the SLICING DISC and use to slice the onions. Put in a saucepan, add the milk and bay leaf and bring to the boil. Cover and simmer for 10 minutes. Strain the milk into a jug, reserve the onions and discard the bay leaf. Butter an ovenproof dish and put in the onions.

Melt the butter in a small pan and, when foaming, stir in the flour. Cook for 2 minutes. Gradually add the milk and bring to the boil, stirring continuously. Cook until thick and smooth. Add a very little salt, some pepper and nutmeg. Pour over the onions. Sprinkle the nuts evenly over the top. Bake in a moderately hot oven (190°C/375°F, Gas Mark 5) for 20 to 30 minutes, reducing heat if the nuts are browning too quickly. Serve garnished with tomatoes and parsley.
Serves 2

VEGETABLE CHEESE PIE

Metric/Imperial	American
100 g/4 oz Gruyère or Emmenthal cheese	¼ lb Gruyère or Emmenthal cheese
450 g/1 lb potatoes, peeled and parboiled	1 lb potatoes, peeled and parboiled
225 g/8 oz mushrooms, wiped	2 cups mushrooms, wiped
450 g/1 lb ripe tomatoes, peeled, or 1 × 400 g/14 oz can tomatoes, roughly chopped	1 lb ripe tomatoes, peeled, or a 1 × 14 oz can tomatoes, roughly chopped
225 g/8 oz cooked peas	1½ cup cooked peas
salt	salt
freshly ground black pepper	freshly ground black pepper
1 tablespoon snipped chives or ½ teaspoon dried	1 tablespoon snipped chives or ½ teaspoon dried
6 fresh basil leaves or ¼ teaspoon dried	6 fresh basil leaves or ¼ teaspoon dried
4 eggs	4 eggs
150 ml/¼ pint single cream	⅔ cup light cream

Fit the SLICING DISC. Slice the cheese and set aside. Slice the potatoes and set aside. Slice the mushrooms and set aside.

In a greased deep pie dish make layers of the potatoes, mushrooms, chopped tomatoes, peas, and cheese slices, seasoning well between layers with the salt and pepper.

Fit the METAL BLADE. If fresh chives and basil are used, chop finely. Feed fresh or dried herbs with eggs and cream through feed tube and blend for 30 seconds. Pour over the vegetables and bake in a moderate oven (180°C/350°F, Gas Mark 4) until brown and bubbling.

Serves 6

BAKED CELERIAC CREAM

Metric/Imperial	American
1 large celeriac, peeled and quartered	1 large celeriac, peeled and quartered
lemon juice	lemon juice
75 g/3 oz Emmenthal cheese	3 oz Emmenthal cheese
2 eggs, separated	2 eggs, separated
salt	salt
freshly ground black pepper	freshly ground black pepper
toasted flaked almonds, to garnish	toasted flaked almonds, to garnish
tomato sauce (page 48), to serve	tomato sauce (page 48), to serve

Cook the celeriac in boiling salted water with a little lemon juice added, until tender, about 25 minutes. Drain well.

Fit the GRATING DISC and grate the cheese, set aside. Fit the METAL BLADE. Put the celeriac into the bowl and process until smooth. Add the egg yolks, cheese and salt and pepper and process until well blended using pulse action. Pour into a large bowl.

Whisk the whites with a few grains of salt until stiff but not dry. Stir 2 tablespoons of the whites into the celeriac mixture. Adjust the seasoning, then fold in the remaining whites. Pour into a greased ovenproof dish and bake in a moderate oven (180°C/350°F, Gas Mark 4) for 45 minutes or until just firm. Sprinkle with the almonds and serve with Tomato Sauce (omit the prawns/shrimp from the recipe on page 48).

Serves 4

COURGETTE (ZUCCHINI) AND MUSHROOM SMITAINE

Metric/Imperial	American
3 slices fresh bread, crusts removed	3 slices fresh bread, crusts removed
450 g/1 lb courgettes, trimmed	1 lb zucchini, trimmed
1 clove garlic, crushed	1 clove garlic, crushed
½ teaspoon dried dill	½ teaspoon dried dill
salt	salt
75 g/3 oz butter	¼ cup plus 2 tablespoons butter
225 g/8 oz firm button mushrooms	2 cups firm button mushrooms
25 g/1 oz flour	¼ cup flour
250 ml/8 fl oz soured cream	1 cup sour cream
freshly ground black pepper	freshly ground black pepper
TO GARNISH:	TO GARNISH:
peeled tomato wedges	peeled tomato wedges
watercress sprigs	watercress sprigs

Fit the METAL BLADE. Put the bread into the bowl and process to fine crumbs, using pulse action, set aside. Fit the SLICING DISC and use to slice the courgettes (zucchini).

Put the courgettes (zucchini) into a saucepan with the garlic and dill. Cover with boiling water, salt lightly and simmer gently until tender. Drain, and reserve 2 tablespoons of the liquid.

Melt 25 g/1 oz/2 tablespoons of the butter, add the mushrooms and sauté for a few minutes. Stir in the flour and cook for 2 minutes. Add the cream, pepper, reserved liquid and courgettes (zucchini) and slowly bring just to the boil. Adjust the seasoning. Turn into a heated casserole dish and keep hot.

Melt the remaining butter in a small pan and when foaming, tip in the breadcrumbs and sauté until golden and crisp. Sprinkle evenly over the top of the casserole. Serve garnished with tomato and watercress.

This is a good vegetarian dish which can also be served as an accompaniment to roast or grilled (broiled) meat or fish.

Serves 4 to 6

PAN HAGGERTY

Metric/Imperial	American
100 g/4 oz Cheddar cheese, slightly stale and roughly cut up	¼ lb Cheddar cheese, slightly stale and roughly cut up
450 g/1 lb potatoes, peeled and cut into tube-size pieces	1 lb potatoes, peeled and cut into tube-size pieces
225 g/8 oz onions, peeled	½ lb onions, peeled
50 g/2 oz butter or margarine	4 tablespoons butter or margarine
1 teaspoon paprika	1 teaspoon paprika
1 teaspoon dried chervil	1 teaspoon dried chervil
salt	salt
freshly ground black pepper	freshly ground black pepper

Fit the GRATING DISC and use to grate the cheese. Reserve 2 tablespoons and set aside with the other cheese. Fit the SLICING DISC. Slice the potatoes and set aside, then slice the onions and set aside.

Melt the butter or margarine in a large heavy frying pan (skillet). Make layers of the potatoes, onions and cheese in the pan (skillet) ending with a potato layer. Season each layer well with paprika, chervil, salt and pepper. Cover the pan (skillet) with a lid or foil and cook over a low heat for about 40 minutes or until all the vegetables are cooked. Sprinkle the top with the remaining cheese and brown quickly under the grill (broiler). Serve cut in wedges with a green salad.

Serves 4

SAUCES, SALAD DRESSINGS & PRESERVES

For many people with a love of food, the making of a sauce or salad dressing is done with special care and attention. Creating the perfect taste and consistency to enhance a food can be the highlight of a meal.

To other people, making any salad dressing or classic sauce is a daunting prospect. The traditional repertoire of stocks, glazes, broths and essences (extracts) available to the professional chef appear out of reach of the domestic kitchen and cook. Somewhere along the way there is help for all.

With a food processor, emulsion sauces such as Mayonnaise or Special Herb Vinaigrette become easy. The blending and combining are no longer arm-tiring jobs, instead a few bursts of pulse action will produce a smooth textured sauce.

Savoury butters, emulsion sauces and salad dressings are all made in seconds and most can be stored in the refrigerator as there is no last minute attention needed.
Making preserves is usually a time-consuming job, involving lots of cutting and slicing. The food processor can speedily slice all the fruit that goes into marmalade and chop or slice all the vegetables that go into a chutney. Even if one stage of cooking can be hastened it all helps the busy cook and as the recipes in this chapter show the processor takes most of the hard work out of preparing sauces, dressings or preserves.

Summer Marmalade
(page 56)

MAYONNAISE

Metric/Imperial	American
2 egg yolks	2 egg yolks
1 teaspoon dry mustard	1 teaspoon dry mustard
1 teaspoon salt	1 teaspoon salt
¼ teaspoon freshly ground black pepper	¼ teaspoon freshly ground black pepper
pinch cayenne pepper	pinch cayenne pepper
2–4 tablespoons lemon juice or cider or white wine vinegar	2–4 tablespoons lemon juice or cider or white wine vinegar
300 ml/½ pint good salad oil (olive, groundnut, safflower)	1¼ cups good salad oil (olive, peanut, safflower)

Fit the PLASTIC BLADE. Put the egg yolks, mustard, salt, pepper and cayenne, and half the lemon juice or vinegar in the processor bowl. Using pulse action, blend with 2 or 3 bursts. Gradually add the oil through the feed tube with the machine switched on. Add the oil steadily in a thin stream until the mayonnaise thickens. Turn the machine off occasionally to scrape down the bowl and check the consistency. Switch off. Add the remaining lemon juice or vinegar, and with pulse action blend for 2 seconds more.
Makes 300 ml/½ pint/1¼ cups

Variations

GREEN MAYONNAISE

Fit the METAL BLADE. Before making the mayonnaise, finely chop about 6 washed and dried parsley sprigs with a handful of washed, dried watercress leaves in the processor. Remove and set aside. Make mayonnaise as above, remove from bowl and stir in the parsley and watercress.

TARTARE SAUCE

Fit the METAL BLADE. Finely chop 2 or 3 small gherkins (sweet dill pickles) and 2 tablespoons capers. Mix with the mayonnaise, made as above, and serve with fish.

AÏOLI

To the prepared mayonnaise add 1 or 2 cloves garlic, crushed. Serve with crisp raw vegetables.

SPEEDY HOLLANDAISE SAUCE

Metric/Imperial	American
225 g/8 oz butter	1 cup butter
4 egg yolks	4 egg yolks
2 tablespoons lemon juice	2 tablespoons lemon juice
¼ teaspoon salt	¼ teaspoon salt
good pinch cayenne pepper	good pinch cayenne pepper

In a heavy saucepan heat the butter until it is melted and hot. Do not let it brown. Fit the PLASTIC BLADE.
Put the egg yolks in the processor bowl with the lemon juice, salt and cayenne, blend with 3 or 4 bursts of pulse action. Pour the hot butter through the feed tube, with machine switched on, in a steady stream. Switch off when all the butter has been added. Serve warm but not hot with asparagus, Brussels sprouts, leeks or poached eggs on toast.
Makes about 250 ml/8 fl oz/1 cup

TOMATO AND PRAWN (SHRIMP) SAUCE

Metric/Imperial	American
1 onion, peeled and quartered	1 onion, peeled and quartered
1 carrot, scraped and cut into pieces	1 carrot, scraped and cut into pieces
1 celery stick, cut into pieces	1 celery stick, cut into pieces
1 leek, cleaned and cut into pieces	1 leek, cleaned and cut into pieces
50 g/2 oz butter	¼ cup butter
1 × 400 g/14 oz can tomatoes	1 × 14 oz can tomatoes
1 clove garlic, crushed	1 clove garlic, crushed
250 ml/8 fl oz strong beef stock or ½ stock cube and water	1 cup strong beef stock or ½ bouillon cube and water
2 teaspoons tomato purée	2 teaspoons tomato paste
½ teaspoon dried basil	½ teaspoon dried basil
bouquet garni	bouquet garni
pinch of sugar	pinch of sugar
salt	salt
freshly ground black pepper	freshly ground black pepper
175 g/6 oz peeled prawns	1 cup peeled shrimp
2 tablespoons parsley sprigs	2 tablespoons parsley sprigs

Fit the METAL BLADE. Place the onion, carrot, celery and leek into the bowl and process until finely chopped.

Melt the butter in a large pan, add the vegetables and allow them to sweat for 15 minutes. Add the tomatoes and juice, the garlic, beef stock, tomato purée (paste), basil, bouquet garni, sugar, salt and pepper. Bring to the boil, stirring, then cover and simmer for 1 hour. Remove the bouquet garni.

Pour the sauce into the processor bowl and process until smooth. Adjust the seasoning. Stir in the prawns (shrimp) and parsley (chopped in the processor). Serve chilled. The sauce can be served hot, omitting the prawns (shrimp).

Makes 600 ml/1 pint/2½ cups

SAUCE BÉARNAISE

Metric/Imperial	American
3 shallots, peeled and quartered	3 shallots, peeled and quartered
3 sprigs fresh tarragon, leaves only, or 1 teaspoon dried tarragon	3 sprigs fresh tarragon, leaves only, or 1 teaspoon dried tarragon
4 tablespoons tarragon vinegar	4 tablespoons tarragon vinegar
salt	salt
freshly ground white pepper	freshly ground white pepper
3 egg yolks	3 egg yolks
225 g/8 oz unsalted butter	1 cup sweet butter

Put the shallots, tarragon, vinegar and a little salt and pepper into a small pan. Bring to the boil then simmer until reduced to 1 tablespoon. Remove from the heat and stir in 1 tablespoon of cold water.

Fit the METAL BLADE. Strain the mixture and place into the bowl. Add the egg yolks and give 1 burst of pulse action. Melt the butter in a small pan. Pour the butter through the feed tube with the machine switched on. Turn the machine off as soon as all the butter is added. Transfer the sauce to a small bowl and adjust the seasoning. Cover with buttered paper and keep warm in a pan of warm water. This sauce is always served warm, never hot or cold.

Makes 250 ml/8 fl oz/1 cup

Variation

SAUCE VALOISE

To the above quantity of Béarnaise Sauce, add 1 teaspoon beef extract. Stir through just before adjusting the seasoning.

BUTTERED ALMOND SAUCE

Metric/Imperial	American
50 g/2 oz blanched almonds	½ cup blanched almonds
75 g/3 oz butter	¼ cup plus 2 tablespoons butter
1 spring onion, finely sliced	1 scallion, finely sliced
juice of ½ a small lemon	juice of ½ a small lemon
salt	salt
freshly ground pepper	freshly ground pepper

Fit the GRATING DISC. Put the almonds into the feed tube and grate, pushing through with the pusher.

Melt the butter in a small pan and stir in the almonds. Cook gently until they are golden. Add the onion (scallion) and lemon juice and season to taste.

Serve hot with fish dishes.

Serves 4

APPLE CREAM SAUCE

Metric/Imperial	American
450 g/1 lb cooking apples, peeled, cored and quartered	1 lb baking apples, peeled, cored and quartered
50 g/2 oz granulated sugar	¼ cup sugar
120 ml/4 fl oz white wine	½ cup white wine
1 tablespoon mayonnaise	1 tablespoon mayonnaise
1 tablespoon horseradish sauce	1 tablespoon horseradish sauce
salt	salt
freshly ground white pepper	freshly ground white pepper

Fit the SLICING DISC. Pack the apples into the feed tube and slice. Put the apples, sugar and wine into a saucepan and cook over a gentle heat until the apples 'fall' and are tender. Increase the heat and cook until the liquid is reduced. Cool.

Fit the PLASTIC BLADE. Pour the apples into the bowl and process until smooth. Add the mayonnaise, horseradish and salt and pepper and blend, using pulse action.

Serve chilled with cold pork and bacon (ham) dishes.

Makes 300 ml/½ pint/1¼ cups

From left front clockwise:
Apple Cream Sauce,
Buttered Almond Sauce,
Spanish Sauce and Creole Sauce

SPANISH SAUCE

Metric/Imperial	American
1 large onion, peeled and quartered	1 large onion, peeled and quartered
1 small green pepper, seeded and quartered	1 small green pepper, seeded and quartered
50 g/2 oz stuffed olives	$\frac{1}{3}$ cup stuffed olives
1 clove garlic, crushed	1 clove garlic, crushed
40 g/1½ oz butter	3 tablespoons butter
1 × 400 g/14 oz can tomatoes	1 × 14 oz can tomatoes
pinch of ground cloves	pinch of ground cloves
salt	salt
freshly ground black pepper	freshly ground black pepper
1 bay leaf	1 bay leaf

Fit the METAL BLADE. Place the onion, pepper, olives, and garlic into the processor bowl and finely chop.

Melt the butter in a saucepan, add the vegetables and sauté until golden. Drain the tomatoes, reserving juice. Slice thickly and add to the pan with the juice. Stir in the cloves, salt and pepper and the bay leaf. Bring to the boil. Reduce heat and simmer until thick, about 25 minutes. Remove bay leaf.

Serve with poultry, meat, fish and omelettes.

Makes 450 ml/¾ pint/2 cups

CREOLE MAYONNAISE

Metric/Imperial	American
1 small onion, peeled and quartered	1 small onion, peeled and quartered
4 anchovy fillets, drained	4 anchovy fillets, drained
1 tablespoon capers	1 tablespoon capers
1 small green pepper, seeded and cut into pieces	1 small green pepper, seeded and cut into pieces
1 tablespoon parsley sprigs	1 tablespoon parsley sprigs
2 teaspoons curry paste	2 teaspoons curry paste
pinch of cayenne pepper	pinch of cayenne pepper
1 tablespoon tomato purée	1 tablespoon tomato paste
300 ml/½ pint mayonnaise (page 48)	1¼ cups mayonnaise (page 48)

Fit the METAL BLADE. Place the onion, anchovies, capers, green pepper and parsley into the bowl and process until finely chopped. Add the remaining ingredients and process, using pulse action, until blended. Pour into a small bowl, cover and chill.

Serve with hot and cold shellfish dishes.

Makes about 300 ml/½ pint/1¼ cups

CURRY SAUCE

Metric/Imperial	American
25 g/1 oz blanched almonds	¼ cup blanched almonds
1 small onion, peeled and halved	1 small onion, peeled and halved
40 g/1½ oz butter	3 tablespoons butter
1 tablespoon curry powder or to taste	1 tablespoon curry powder or to taste
1 tablespoon flour	1 tablespoon flour
150 ml/¼ pint tomato juice	⅔ cup tomato juice
salt	salt
freshly ground black pepper	freshly ground black pepper
300 ml/½ pint water	1¼ cups water
1 tablespoon lemon juice	1 tablespoon lemon juice
2 teaspoons sugar	2 teaspoons sugar
3 tablespoons natural yogurt	3 tablespoons unflavored yogurt

Fit the METAL BLADE. Put the almonds in the processor bowl and process to a fine texture. Remove and set aside. Put the onions into the processor bowl and process until finely chopped.

Melt the butter in a heavy saucepan and sauté the onion until it is a pale gold colour. Stir in the curry powder, flour, tomato juice, salt and pepper and water. Add the almonds, bring to the boil and stir in the lemon juice and sugar. Simmer for a few minutes until thickened.

Pour the sauce into the processor bowl and process to a smooth purée. Reheat, adjust seasoning, and stir in the yogurt. Serve with meatballs, reheated cooked meat, hard-boiled (cooked) eggs or vegetables.

Serves 4

SESAME SEED DRESSING

Metric/Imperial	American
150 ml/¼ pint sesame seed oil	⅔ cup sesame seed oil
1 large clove garlic, crushed	1 large clove garlic, crushed
2 teaspoons sesame seeds	2 teaspoons sesame seeds
1 tablespoon wine vinegar (or more if a sharp dressing is preferred)	1 tablespoon wine vinegar (or more if a sharp dressing is preferred)
salt	salt
freshly ground black pepper	freshly ground black pepper

Put the oil into a small pan and add the garlic and sesame seeds. Heat very gently until the seeds turn golden. Strain the oil into a heatproof jug and mix the seeds and garlic with the vinegar. Cool the oil.

Fit the PLASTIC BLADE. Add salt and pepper to the garlic mixture (not too much) and place in the processor bowl. Switch the machine on and pour the oil through the feed tube. Process for a few seconds or until the dressing thickens. Adjust the seasoning. Store in a covered jar in the refrigerator.

Use in place of French dressing.

Makes 150 ml/¼ pint/⅔ cup

CHILLED GARLIC CREAM DRESSING

Metric/Imperial	American
120 ml/4 fl oz soured cream	½ cup sour cream
2 tablespoons single cream	2 tablespoons light cream
2 tablespoons mayonnaise	2 tablespoons mayonnaise
3 large cloves garlic, crushed	3 large cloves garlic, crushed
1 tablespoon white wine vinegar, or to taste	1 tablespoon white wine vinegar, or to taste
2 tablespoons salad oil	2 tablespoons salad oil
pinch of sugar	pinch of sugar
salt	salt
freshly ground white pepper	freshly ground white pepper

Fit the METAL BLADE. Put all the ingredients into the bowl and process until smooth. Pour into a small bowl and adjust the seasoning. Cover and chill. Allow the dressing to mature for about 1 hour before using.

Makes approximately 250 ml/8 fl oz/1 cup

SPECIAL HERB VINAIGRETTE

Metric/Imperial	American
2 sprigs each of chervil, tarragon and dill, washed	2 sprigs each of chervil, tarragon, and dill, washed
25 g/1 oz parsley sprigs, washed	1/4 cup parsley sprigs, washed
2 tablespoons tarragon vinegar	2 tablespoons tarragon vinegar
1 teaspoon Dijon mustard	1 teaspoon Dijon mustard
salt	salt
freshly ground black pepper	freshly ground black pepper
250 ml/8 fl oz olive or salad oil	1 cup olive or salad oil
1 tablespoon snipped chives	1 tablespoon snipped chives

Place the herbs on kitchen paper towels and dry. Fit the METAL BLADE.

Put the herbs into the bowl, add the vinegar, mustard and a little salt and pepper. Process until coarsely chopped. With the machine on, pour the oil through the feed tube, processing until the herbs are finely chopped and the dressing is combined. Adjust the seasoning. Remove and stir in the chives.

This is an excellent dressing for fish, eggs or a green salad.

Makes 250 ml/8 fl oz/1 cup

HOMEMADE SALAD CREAM

Metric/Imperial	American
3 tablespoons plain flour	3 tablespoons all-purpose flour
1 tablespoon caster sugar	1 tablespoon sugar
2 teaspoons dry mustard	2 teaspoons dry mustard
1 teaspoon salt	1 teaspoon salt
150 ml/1/4 pint milk	2/3 cup milk
2 eggs	2 eggs
50 g/2 oz butter, cut into pieces	1/4 cup butter, cut into pieces
3 tablespoons cider vinegar	3 tablespoons cider vinegar
150 ml/1/4 pint groundnut or soya oil	2/3 cup peanut or soya oil

Fit the PLASTIC BLADE. Place the flour, sugar, mustard and salt in the bowl and blend, using 2 or 3 bursts of pulse action. Pour in the milk and blend quickly.

Pour into a saucepan and bring to the boil, stirring continually. Cook for 1 minute and cool slightly. Return to the food processor. Add the eggs and butter and blend with 3 or 4 bursts of pulse action. Add the vinegar and oil and blend again. Pour back into the saucepan and heat gently, stirring continuously, until thick. Do not boil.

This salad cream keeps well in a covered container in the refrigerator and does not separate or go oily.

Makes 450 ml/3/4 pint/2 cups

CUMBERLAND RUM BUTTER

Metric/Imperial	American
225 g/8 oz unsalted butter	1 cup sweet butter
350 g/12 oz dark soft brown sugar	2 cups brown sugar
120 ml/4 fl oz Jamaican rum	1/2 cup Jamaican rum
2 teaspoons grated nutmeg	2 teaspoons grated nutmeg
sifted icing sugar, to decorate	sifted confectioners' sugar, to decorate

Fit the METAL BLADE. Place all the ingredients, except the icing (confectioners') sugar, into the bowl and process until light and fluffy, scraping down the bowl once or twice. Put into an attractive china dish and dust with a little sifted icing (confectioners') sugar.

Serve with Christmas pudding and mince pies or, as they do in the north of England, spread on plain sweet biscuits (cookies).

Makes approximately 450 g/1 lb

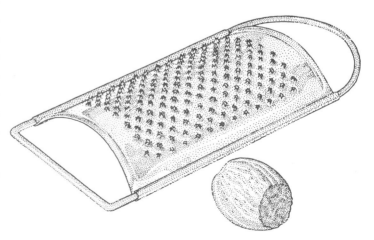

CRÈME PÂTISSIÈRE

Metric/Imperial	American
50 g/2 oz caster sugar	½ cup sugar
2 egg yolks	2 egg yolks
1½ tablespoons plain flour	1½ tablespoons all-purpose flour
1 teaspoon cornflour	1 teaspoon cornstarch
300 ml/½ pint milk	1¼ cups milk
½ teaspoon vanilla essence	½ teaspoon vanilla extract

Fit the METAL BLADE. Blend the sugar, egg yolks, flour, cornflour (cornstarch) and 2 tablespoons of the milk. Heat the remaining milk almost to boiling point. Pour through the feed tube, with the machine on, and blend for 10 seconds.

Put the blended mixture in a saucepan and heat very gently until boiling, stirring all the time. Simmer for 3 minutes until the mixture thickly coats the back of the spoon. Stir in the vanilla.

This crème pâtissière will keep in the refrigerator. Cover with a circle of wetted greaseproof (wax) paper cut to fit inside the bowl and then lid with cling film (plastic wrap). Do not freeze.

Makes 300 ml/½ pint/1¼ cups

ALMOND VELVET

Metric/Imperial	American
75 g/3 oz blanched almonds	½ cup blanched almonds
50 g/2 oz icing sugar	½ cup confectioners' sugar
40 g/1½ oz butter or margarine, softened	3 tablespoons butter or margarine, softened
1 egg	1 egg
1 tablespoon cornflour	1 tablespoon cornstarch
1 tablespoon rum or ½ teaspoon vanilla essence	1 tablespoon rum or ½ teaspoon vanilla extract

Fit the METAL BLADE. Chop the almonds very finely (but do not process to a powder). Remove and set aside. Place the butter and sugar in the bowl and blend. Add the almonds through the feed tube, drop in the egg and blend for 30 seconds only. Add the cornflour (cornstarch) and rum or vanilla and blend using 4 or 5 bursts of pulse action. Refrigerate in a tightly closed container for up to three weeks.

Use almond velvet as a filling for Swiss (jelly) rolls, sponge (layer) cakes or in split panels of cooked puff pastry.

Makes 175 g/6 oz

From left: Almond Velvet and Almond Paste (Marzipan)

HALF-PRICE CREAM

Metric/Imperial	American
1½ teaspoons gelatine	1½ teaspoons unflavored gelatin
300 ml/½ pint milk	1¼ cups milk
225 g/8 oz unsalted butter	1 cup sweet butter

Fit the PLASTIC BLADE. Soften the gelatine in 5 tablespoons of the milk, then dissolve. Heat the remaining milk and butter in a small pan until the butter has melted and the milk is warm.

Put the gelatine and milk mixture in the processor bowl and blend, for about 10 seconds, using pulse action. Refrigerate in a covered container overnight.

Stir and use as you would thick double (heavy) cream. This cream can be whipped gently to soft peak stage.

Makes approximately 450 ml/¾ pint/2 cups

ALMOND PASTE (MARZIPAN)

Metric/Imperial	American
225 g/8 oz ground almonds	2 cups ground almonds
150 g/5 oz caster sugar	⅔ cup sugar
175 g/6 oz icing sugar, sifted	1⅓ cups sifted confectioners' sugar
1 egg yolk	1 egg yolk
1 tablespoon lemon juice	1 tablespoon lemon juice
1 tablespoon brandy or sherry	1 tablespoon brandy or sherry
½ teaspoon vanilla essence	½ teaspoon vanilla extract
1 teaspoon orange flower water (optional)	1 teaspoon orange flower water (optional)

Fit the PLASTIC BLADE. Put the ground almonds and sugars into the processor bowl. Process for 4 seconds. Mix together the remaining ingredients and pour into the bowl. Process until the mixture forms a ball around the blade. Wrap in cling film (plastic wrap) and allow to mature for 24 hours.

Use to cover a fruit cake before icing, to fill stoned (pitted) dates or to make small shapes for decorating a cake.

Makes approximately 450 g/1 lb

CHOCOLATE BRANDY SAUCE

Metric/Imperial	American
100 g/4 oz good dark chocolate, broken into pieces	4 squares good semi-sweet chocolate, broken into pieces
150 ml/¼ pint double cream	⅔ cup heavy cream
1 tablespoon brandy	1 tablespoon brandy

Fit the GRATING DISC. Grate the chocolate and reserve.

Heat the cream in a small pan and bring gently to the boil. Remove from the heat and stir in the chocolate. Stir until the chocolate has melted then stir in the brandy. Serve hot or cold. The sauce thickens as it cools.

Serve with ice cream and hot or cold soufflés.

Makes 300 ml/½ pint/1¼ cups

LIME MARMALADE

Metric/Imperial	American
8 large green limes (when yellow they are too ripe)	8 large green limes (when yellow they are too ripe)
water	water
preserving sugar	sugar

Peel the limes very thinly, making sure that no pith is on the peel. Finely shred the peel using a sharp knife. Remove all the pith and put in a muslin (cheesecloth) bag. Roughly chop the fruit and remove the seeds (pits). Place the seeds (pits) in the muslin (cheesecloth) bag and tie.

Fit the METAL BLADE. Place the fruit in the processor bowl and process until smooth. Combine the pulp and peel and measure. Put in a large bowl with 3 times the quantity of water. Add the muslin (cheesecloth) bag and leave to stand overnight.

Put into a large pan and bring to the boil. Simmer until the peel is soft. Measure the liquid again and for each 600 ml/1 pint/2½ cups of liquid add the same amount of sugar. Heat very gently to dissolve the sugar then boil slowly until the marmalade reaches setting point. To test for setting point, dip a wooden spoon into the marmalade and allow to cool slightly until a thin skin forms. Pour back into the pan, the marmalade is ready if it forms a large blob to run off the spoon. Pour into sterilized, hot, dry jars. Cool, cover and label.

Makes approximately 1.75 kg/4 lb

SUMMER MARMALADE

Metric/Imperial	American
1 large grapefruit	1 large grapefruit
2 lemons	2 lemons
1 large thin-skinned orange	1 large thin-skinned orange
water	water
preserving sugar	sugar
1 tablespoon black treacle	1 tablespoon molasses

Fit the SLICING DISC. Wash the fruit and remove the blossom ends. Roughly cut the fruit into tube-size pieces. Remove pips (pits), put into a muslin (cheesecloth) bag and tie with a piece of string. Feed the fruit into the feed tube and slice. Weigh the peel and pulp. Put the fruit in a large basin with 3 times its weight in water, and the bag of pips (pits). Leave to stand at room temperature for 24 hours.

In a large enamel-lined saucepan, simmer fruit and water until reduced to half its original quantity. Weigh and return to the pan. Add an equal weight of sugar less 100 g/4 oz/¼ lb. Stir in the black treacle (molasses). Bring slowly to the boil, stirring often until the sugar dissolves. Bring to a rolling boil, without stirring, and cook until a sugar thermometer registers 100°C/212°F.

Remove the bag of pips (pits). Remove marmalade from heat. Test for setting by dropping a teaspoon of marmalade onto a chilled saucer. Let it cool and push gently with a fingertip. If it wrinkles the marmalade is ready. If not, boil more and repeat the testing process, using either a sugar thermometer or the saucer test.

Leave to stand for 30 minutes, stirring once or twice. Ladle into sterilized, hot, dry jars. Cool, seal, label and keep in a cool, dark place.

Makes approximately 2.5 kg/6 lb marmalade

GREEN TOMATO CHUTNEY

Metric/Imperial	American
450 g/1 lb onions, peeled and quartered	1 lb onions, peeled and quartered
2 kg/4 lb green tomatoes, peeled	4 lb green tomatoes, peeled
450 g/1 lb apples, peeled and cored	1 lb apples, peeled and cored
1 teaspoon salt	1 teaspoon salt
900 ml–1.2 litres/1½–2 pints cider vinegar	3¾–5 cups cider vinegar
1 teaspoon ground ginger	1 teaspoon ground ginger
1 teaspoon mild curry powder	1 teaspoon mild curry powder
450 g/1 lb soft dark or light brown sugar	2⅔ cups light brown sugar

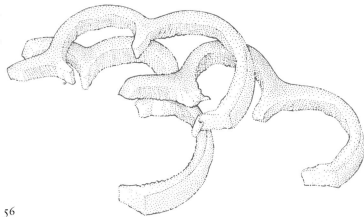

Fit the SLICING DISC and use to slice the onions. Place the onions in large enamel-lined saucepan. Cut the tomatoes into tube-size pieces, if necessary, and slice. Add the tomatoes to the onion. Cut the apples into tube-size pieces and slice. Add to the pan, with the salt and 300 ml/½ pint/1¼ cups of the vinegar. Bring to the boil and simmer until the tomato and apples are soft.

Add the ginger, curry powder, sugar and remaining vinegar and simmer, stirring occasionally until the mixture is thick. Add more vinegar to taste, if liked.

Pack into sterilized hot, dry jars and seal.

Makes approximately 2.5 kg/6 lb chutney

BANANA CHUTNEY

Metric/Imperial	American
450 g/1 lb Spanish onions, peeled and cut into pieces	1 lb Bermuda onions, peeled and cut into pieces
225 g/8 oz stoned dates	1 cup pitted dates
6 bananas, peeled and cut into pieces	6 bananas, peeled and cut into pieces
300 ml/½ pint vinegar	1¼ cups vinegar
100 g/4 oz crystallized ginger, sliced	¼ lb sliced candied ginger
1 teaspoon curry powder	1 teaspoon curry powder
225 g/8 oz black treacle	1 cup (½ lb) molasses
1–2 teaspoons salt	1–2 teaspoons salt

Fit the METAL BLADE. Separately process the onions and dates until finely chopped. Put both into an enamel-lined saucepan. Process the bananas to a purée and add to the pan. Pour over the vinegar and bring to the boil. Reduce the heat and simmer until tender, about 15 minutes. Stir in the remaining ingredients adding the salt last, to see how much is needed. Simmer until the chutney is rich and brown. Pour into sterilized hot dry jars and seal.

Makes approximately 1.5 kg/3 lb chutney.

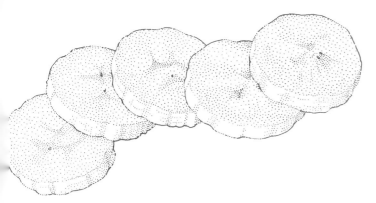

FRESH CHUTNEY

Metric/Imperial	American
1 medium onion, peeled and quartered	1 medium onion, peeled and quartered
175 g/6 oz cooking apples, cored	6 oz baking apples, cored
grated rind and juice of 1 lemon	grated rind and juice of 1 lemon
cider vinegar	cider vinegar

Fit the METAL BLADE. Put onion in the processor bowl and process until very finely chopped. Remove and weigh. The recipe requires 75 g/3 oz finely chopped onion. Roughly chop apples using 2 or 3 bursts of pulse action. Mix the onion, apple, lemon rind and juice with just enough vinegar to moisten. Spoon into a clean glass jar and seal. Keep refrigerated and use within 2 weeks.

Makes approximately 275 g/10 oz chutney

Variation

Add 1 tablespoon finely chopped preserved ginger or 2 tablespoons desiccated coconut to the apple mixture before adding the cider.

PEPPER RELISH

Metric/Imperial	American
6 sweet red peppers, seeded and cut into pieces	6 sweet red peppers, seeded and cut into pieces
6 green peppers, seeded and cut into pieces	6 green peppers, seeded and cut into pieces
6 onions, peeled and quartered	6 onions, peeled and quartered
3 cloves garlic, crushed	3 cloves garlic, crushed
250 ml/8 fl oz vinegar	1 cup vinegar
175 g/6 oz soft brown sugar	1 cup light brown sugar
1 tablespoon salt	1 tablespoon salt
1 tablespoon celery seeds	1 tablespoon celery seeds
few drops Tabasco sauce	few drops Tabasco sauce

Fit the GRATING DISC and use to grate the peppers and onions. Put the grated vegetables into a sieve and pour boiling water over them. Place all the ingredients into a saucepan and bring to the boil. Reduce heat and simmer for 30 minutes. Pour into sterilized hot, dry jars and seal.

Makes about 2 kg/4½ lb relish

LIGHT MEALS

Weekends and holidays seem to be made for serving light meals. With all the family either out or rushing about, a quickly prepared light meal that will sustain them is needed. Build up a good supply of short cut ingredients (page 119) and you have the makings of many light meals, be it pancakes (crêpes) or a cheese, bacon and herb omelette. Light meals seems to cover all times, whether a late breakfast, lunch, early tea or dinner and your food processor can be used to make them all.

In this section the recipe for Egg and Bacon Nests would be quite suitable for a late breakfast.

Italian Eggs, served on a bed of tomatoes and garnished with parsley is a colourful yet simple meal to serve on a pleasant spring day, bringing with it memories of the previous summer's holiday, perhaps spent in the sun.

When on holiday, meals eaten out of doors seem to taste even better. A tart or vegetable flan (see pages 61 and 63) with a green salad, white wine and a wedge of cheese to follow is practically unbeatable.

When the weather closes in a hot meal consisting of a hearty soup with Savoury French Stick (page 64), served around a roaring open fire, is a delightful and relaxed way to eat.

Onion Cream Tart
(page 60)

ONION CREAM TART

Metric/Imperial	American
225 g/8 oz shortcrust pastry (page 101)	½ lb basic pie dough (page 101)
750 g/1½ lb onions, peeled	1½ lb onions, peeled
25 g/1 oz butter	2 tablespoons butter
2 tablespoons olive oil	2 tablespoons olive oil
1 clove garlic, crushed	1 clove garlic, crushed
1 egg	1 egg
1 egg yolk	1 egg yolk
4 tablespoons double cream	¼ cup heavy cream
freshly ground black pepper	freshly ground black pepper
12 anchovy fillets	12 anchovy fillets
12 black olives, stoned	12 ripe olives, pitted
TO GARNISH:	TO GARNISH:
lemon twist	lemon twist
parsley	parsley
watercress sprigs	watercress sprigs

Roll out the pastry (pie dough) on a floured board and use to line a 20 cm/8 inch flan tin (pie pan). Prick the bottom with a fork and put in the refrigerator to chill. Fit the SLICING DISC and slice the onions.

Melt the butter and oil in a saucepan. Add the onions, cover and allow to cook very gently until they are soft and golden. Do not hurry this process which should take about 45 minutes. Stir in the garlic. Place in the pastry case (pie shell).

Beat together the egg and egg yolk, cream and a little black pepper. Pour over the onions. Arrange the anchovies in a lattice over the top and place an olive in each square.

Bake in a moderately hot oven (200°C/400°F, Gas Mark 6) for 20 minutes, then reduce the temperature to 180°C/350°F, Gas Mark 4, for a further 15 minutes. Transfer to a serving dish and garnish with the lemon and a few parsley and watercress sprigs.

This tart is best served warm but it is good cold for picnics and lunch boxes.
Serves 6

EGG AND BACON NESTS

Metric/Imperial	American
2 slices bread, crusts removed and torn into pieces	2 slices bread, crusts removed and torn into pieces
50 g/2 oz Cheddar cheese	2 oz Cheddar cheese
40 g/1½ oz butter	3 tablespoons butter
4 streaky bacon rashers, rinds removed	4 slices fatty bacon, rinds removed
4 eggs	4 eggs
salt	salt
freshly ground black pepper	freshly ground black pepper
parsley, to garnish	parsley, to garnish

Fit the METAL BLADE. Put the bread into the bowl and process to fine crumbs. Set aside. Fit the GRATING DISC and use to grate the cheese. Set aside.

Melt 25 g/1 oz/2 tablespoons of the butter in a small pan, stir in the breadcrumbs and cook gently until golden. Drain on kitchen paper. In the same pan, partially cook the bacon. Grease 4 individual ovenproof dishes with the remaining butter. Mix the crumbs and cheese together and divide between the dishes. Line the sides of each dish with a rasher (slice) of bacon. Break the eggs into the centres and season lightly. Bake in a moderately hot oven (200°C/400°F, Gas Mark 6) for about 8 minutes. The whites should be set and the yolks soft. Serve sprinkled with parsley, chopped in the processor.
Serves 4

HAM, CHEESE AND NOODLE MOULD

Metric/Imperial	American
50 g/2 oz Cheddar cheese	2 oz Cheddar cheese
25 g/1 oz Parmesan cheese, cut into pieces	1 oz Parmesan cheese, cut into pieces
2 slices fresh brown bread, crusts removed and torn into pieces	2 slices fresh brown bread, crusts removed and torn into pieces
100 g/4 oz ham or boiled bacon trimmings	¼ lb cured or boiled ham trimmings
250 g/8 oz ribbon noodles	½ lb ribbon noodles
65 g/2½ oz butter	5 tablespoons butter
2 eggs, beaten	2 eggs, beaten
homemade tomato sauce (page 48) to serve	homemade tomato sauce (page 48) to serve

Fit the GRATING DISC and use to grate the cheese. Set aside. Fit the METAL BLADE. Put the Parmesan cheese in the bowl and process until very fine. Set aside. Put the bread into the bowl and process to fine crumbs. Add to the Parmesan and mix well. Place the ham or bacon trimmings in the bowl and chop coarsely with 2 or 3 bursts of pulse action. Set aside.

Cook the noodles in plenty of boiling salted water, drain well and return to the saucepan. Mix in 50 g/2 oz/¼ cup of the butter to the noodles and shake the pan well, taking care not to break up the noodles. Add the ham or bacon, Cheddar cheese and eggs and shake the pan again. Grease an 18 cm/7 inch soufflé dish with the remaining butter and dust it with the Parmesan cheese and crumbs. Pour in the noodle mixture. Stand the dish in a roasting tin (pan) half filled with hot water. Bake in a moderate oven (180°C/350°F, Gas Mark 4) for 30 minutes. Turn on to a heated serving dish and serve with homemade tomato sauce (omit the prawns/shrimp from the recipe on page 48).

Serves 4

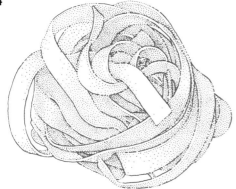

TARTE PESTO

Metric/Imperial	American
225 g/8 oz shortcrust pastry (page 101)	½ lb basic pie dough (page 101)
350 g/12 oz cream cheese	¾ lb cream cheese
2 tablespoons soured cream	2 tablespoons sour cream
2 tablespoons parsley sprigs	2 tablespoons parsley sprigs
1 egg	1 egg
1 egg yolk	1 egg yolk
salt	salt
freshly ground black pepper	freshly ground black pepper
6 tomatoes, peeled, seeded and sliced	6 tomatoes, peeled, seeded and sliced
FOR THE PESTO:	FOR THE PESTO:
15 g/½ oz fresh basil leaves or 2 teaspoons dried	½ oz fresh basil leaves or 2 teaspoons dried
50 g/2 oz pine nuts	½ cup pine nuts
25 g/1 oz parsley sprigs	¼ cup (1 oz) parsley sprigs
25 g/1 oz freshly grated Parmesan cheese	¼ cup freshly grated Parmesan cheese
120 ml/4 fl oz olive oil	½ cup olive oil
salt	salt
freshly ground black pepper	freshly ground black pepper

Roll out the pastry (dough) and use to line a 20 cm/8 inch flan tin (pie pan). Line with greaseproof paper and weigh down with dried beans. Bake blind in a moderately hot oven (200°C/400°F, Gas Mark 6) for 15 minutes. Carefully remove the paper and beans and return to the oven for a further 5 to 10 minutes. Cool. Reduce the oven temperature to moderate (180°C/350°F, Gas Mark 4).

Fit the METAL BLADE. Put the cheese, cream, parsley sprigs, egg and egg yolk, salt and pepper into the bowl. Process until the mixture is smooth and the parsley is finely chopped. Adjust seasoning. Spread half the cheese mixture into the flan case (shell). Arrange half the tomatoes over the top. Cover with the remaining cheese mixture. Smooth the top and cover with the remaining tomato slices. Bake in a moderate oven for 20 minutes or until set.

Put all the ingredients for the Pesto into the processor bowl and process until smooth. Check seasoning. Pour into a small decorative bowl. Serve the tart warm with the Pesto.

Serves 4

VENETIAN FLAN

Metric/Imperial	American
225 g/8 oz shortcrust pastry (page 101)	½ lb basic pie dough (page 101)
50 g/2 oz Gruyère cheese	2 oz Gruyère cheese
75 g/3 oz Cheddar cheese	3 oz Cheddar cheese
1 onion, peeled	1 onion, peeled
1 tablespoon olive oil	1 tablespoon olive oil
225 g/8 oz Italian salami, cut into cubes	½ lb Italian salami, cut into cubes
100 g/4 oz ham, cut into strips	¼ lb ham, cut into strips
3 eggs	3 eggs
300 ml/½ pint top of the milk	1¼ cups top of the milk
salt	salt
freshly ground black pepper	freshly ground black pepper
grated nutmeg	grated nutmeg

Roll out the pastry (pie dough) on a floured board and use to line a 20 cm/8 inch flan tin (pie pan).

Fit the GRATING DISC. Grate the Gruyère and set aside. Grate the Cheddar and set aside. (Keep the cheeses separate.) Fit the slicing disc and slice the onion.

Heat the oil in a frying pan (skillet) and add the onion. Cook gently until soft. Stir in the salami and cook for 5 minutes. Put the onion and salami into the pastry case (pie shell) and sprinkle with half the Gruyère and half the Cheddar. Arrange the ham strips over the top of the cheeses.

In a bowl, beat together the eggs, milk and remaining cheese and add salt, pepper and nutmeg to taste. Pour over the cheese and ham.

Bake in a moderately hot oven (200°C/400°F, Gas Mark 6) for 15 minutes. Reduce heat to 180°C/350°F, Gas Mark 4 and bake for a further 20 minutes or until the custard is set and lightly golden.

Serves 6

COURGETTE (ZUCCHINI) FLAN

Metric/Imperial	American
225 g/8 oz shortcrust pastry (page 101)	½ lb basic pie dough (page 101)
450 g/1 lb courgettes, topped and tailed	1 lb zucchini, topped and tailed
2 eggs	2 eggs
300 ml/½ pint milk	1¼ cups milk
salt	salt
freshly ground black pepper	freshly ground black pepper
grated nutmeg	grated nutmeg
1 clove garlic, crushed	1 clove garlic, crushed
1 teaspoon tomato purée	1 teaspoon tomato paste
dash Tabasco sauce	dash Tabasco sauce

Roll out the pastry (dough) and use to line an 18 cm/7 inch flan tin (pie pan). Line the pastry (dough) with greaseproof (wax) paper and weigh down with dried beans. Bake blind in a moderately hot oven (200°C/400°F, Gas Mark 6) for 15 minutes. Remove foil and beans and bake for a further 5 to 10 minutes. Remove and set aside to cool.

Fit the SLICING DISC and and use to slice the courgettes (zucchini). Blanch in boiling salted water for 1 minute, drain well and set aside.

Fit the PLASTIC BLADE. Process the eggs, milk, salt, pepper, nutmeg, garlic, tomato purée (paste) and Tabasco sauce until well blended. Arrange courgette (zucchini) slices in the pastry case (pie shell). Pour in egg mixture. Bake in a moderately hot oven for 30 to 40 minutes or until set and golden.

Serves 4

ITALIAN EGGS

Metric/Imperial	American
25 g/1 oz parsley sprigs	¼ cup (1 oz) parsley sprigs
1 teaspoon fresh marjoram leaves or a pinch dried	1 teaspoon fresh marjoram leaves or a pinch dried
1 clove garlic, crushed	1 clove garlic, crushed
6 black olives, pitted	6 ripe olives, pitted
1 shallot, peeled	1 shallot, peeled
2 anchovy fillets	2 anchovy fillets
freshly ground black pepper	freshly ground black pepper
120 ml/4 fl oz olive oil	½ cup olive oil
6 hard-boiled eggs, shelled and sliced	6 hard-cooked eggs, shelled and sliced
TO GARNISH:	TO GARNISH:
tomato wedges	tomato wedges
parsley	parsley

Fit the METAL BLADE. Place the parsley, marjoram, garlic, olives, shallot, anchovy fillets and pepper into the bowl and process until smooth. With the machine still running, pour the oil through the feed tube. Adjust the seasoning.

Arrange the eggs on a serving dish and pour the sauce over them. Garnish with tomato wedges and sprinkle with parsley, which has been chopped in the processor.

Serves 4

From left: Italian Eggs, Courgette (Zucchini) Flan and Venetian Flan

STEAMED BACON AND CARROT PUDDING

Metric/Imperial	American
225 g/8 oz carrots, scraped	½ lb carrots, scraped
2 onions, peeled and quartered	2 onions, peeled and quartered
175 g/6 oz self-raising flour	1½ cups self-rising flour
salt	salt
freshly ground black pepper	freshly ground black pepper
50 g/2 oz butter, chilled	¼ cup butter, chilled
1 tablespoon parsley heads	1 tablespoon parsley heads
4 bacon rashers, diced	4 bacon slices, diced
120 ml/4 fl oz chicken stock	½ cup chicken stock
15 g/½ oz sugar	1 tablespoon sugar
½ teaspoon dried thyme	½ teaspoon dried thyme
2 eggs, beaten	2 eggs, beaten
TO GARNISH AND SERVE:	TO GARNISH AND SERVE:
snipped chives	snipped chives
cheese sauce	cheese sauce

Fit the GRATING DISC and use to grate the carrots. Put in a bowl. Fit the METAL BLADE. Process the onions until finely chopped and add to the carrots. Rinse and dry the bowl.

Place the flour, salt, pepper, butter and parsley in the bowl and process to fine crumbs. Add the bacon, stock, sugar, thyme and eggs and process until just mixed using pulse action. Turn into a greased 1.2 litre/2 pint/5 cup pudding basin. Cover with greased paper or foil and tie down with string. Steam for 2 hours. Turn onto a hot dish, sprinkle with chives and serve with cheese sauce.

Serves 4

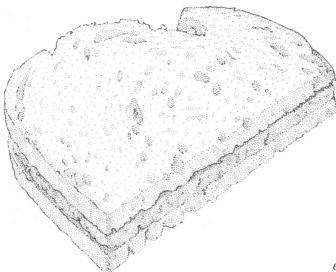

SAVOURY FRENCH STICK

Metric/Imperial	American
100 g/4 oz soft butter	½ cup soft butter
3 tablespoons parsley sprigs	3 tablespoons parsley sprigs
3 tablespoons grated Parmesan cheese	3 tablespoons grated Parmesan cheese
1 clove garlic, crushed	1 clove garlic, crushed
1 tablespoon olive oil	1 tablespoon olive oil
1 teaspoon dried basil	1 teaspoon dried basil
salt	salt
freshly ground black pepper	freshly ground black pepper
1 stick of French bread	1 stick of French bread

Fit the METAL BLADE. Place all the ingredients, except the French bread, into the bowl and process until smooth. Adjust seasoning. Cut the stick crosswise into 3.5 cm/1¼ inch thick slices without cutting through the bottom crust. Spread the mixture between each slice and over the top. Wrap the loaf in foil and put in a moderately hot oven (190°C/375°F, Gas Mark 5) for 20 minutes. Open the foil, and fold back and bake for a further 5 minutes to crisp. Serve with soups or instead of a vegetable.

ORANGE AND WALNUT CHEESE SPREAD

Metric/Imperial	American
50 g/2 oz shelled walnuts	½ cup shelled walnuts
225 g/8 oz cream cheese	1 cup cream cheese
grated rind of 1 large orange	grated rind of 1 large orange
2 spring onions or 1 shallot, peeled and sliced	2 scallions or 1 shallot, peeled and sliced
salt	salt
freshly ground black pepper	freshly ground black pepper

Fit the METAL BLADE. Put the walnuts into the bowl and process until coarsely chopped. Add the cream cheese, orange rind and onions (scallions) or shallot, salt, and pepper. Process until the nuts and onion are finely minced (ground), about 10 seconds.

Use this spread in place of butter when making ham or chicken sandwiches; spread it thickly between plain biscuits (crackers) for the lunch box or use as a dip for crudités.

Makes 275 g/10 oz/1¼ cups

RAREBIT MIX

Metric/Imperial	American
175 g/6 oz mature Cheddar cheese, cut into pieces	6 oz mature Cheddar cheese, cut into pieces
15 g/½ oz self-raising flour	2 tablespoons self-rising flour
1 tablespoon dry mustard	1 tablespoon dry mustard
1 teaspoon Worcestershire sauce	1 teaspoon Worcestershire sauce
1 tablespoon beer, sherry, port or red wine	1 tablespoon beer, sherry, port or red wine
120 ml/4 fl oz milk	½ cup milk
salt	salt
freshly ground black pepper	freshly ground black pepper

Fit the GRATING DISC and use to grate the cheese. Set aside. Fit the PLASTIC BLADE. Place the cheese, flour, mustard, Worcestershire sauce and alcohol in the bowl and season lightly. Bring the milk to the boil, switch machine on, pour milk through the tube and process for 10 seconds. Clean down bowl and process for 5 more seconds. (This mixture will keep in the refrigerator for 3 to 4 days.) To serve, pour over hot toast and grill (broil) until bubbling.
Serves 4

MEAT LOAF FOR SANDWICHES

Metric/Imperial	American
3 slices bread, crusts removed and cut into pieces	3 slices bread, crusts removed and cut into slices
350 g/12 oz chuck steak, trimmed and cut into pieces	¾ lb blade steak, trimmed and cut into pieces
1 onion, peeled and quartered	1 onion, peeled and quartered
100 g/4 oz sausage meat	¼ lb sausage meat
4 tablespoons tomato ketchup	4 tablespoons tomato ketchup
2 teaspoons horseradish sauce	2 teaspoons horseradish sauce
2 teaspoons Worcestershire sauce	2 teaspoons Worcestershire sauce
1 egg, beaten	1 egg, beaten
salt	salt
freshly ground black pepper	freshly ground black pepper

Fit the METAL BLADE. Place the bread in the bowl and process to fine crumbs. Set aside. Process the steak and onion until finely minced (ground). Add the sausage and crumbs and process until mixed, about 6 seconds. Turn the mixture into a bowl. Add 2 tablespoons of the tomato ketchup, the horseradish and Worcestershire sauces, egg and salt and pepper, mix well. Grease a 450 g/1 lb loaf tin (pan). Pack in the meat and spread the remaining ketchup over the top. Bake in a moderately hot oven (200°C/400°F, Gas Mark 6) for 45 minutes. Allow to become completely cold before slicing.
Makes 1 × 450 g/1 lb loaf

MAIN MEALS

With imagination you will find the processor indispensable in the making of many well known classic dishes that demand fine chopping and slicing of several ingredients. Rethink many old favourite recipes and you will save time and effort with the machine. The even slicing and chopping results in even cooking.

For stews and casseroles use the processor to prepare the vegetables in seconds.

A plain grilled (broiled) steak can be enlivened by a sauce or garnish made in the processor. For veal escalopes (cutlets), a garnish made of finely chopped onion, bacon and green pepper is delicious when lightly fried and placed on top of the cooked veal.

Stuffings add body and flavour and are ideal subjects for the chopping and combining action of the processor.

Leftovers can be finely minced (ground) and re-combined to give tasty new variations.

Garnishing is made easy with perfect slices. Presentation of a dish is important, even for a family meal.

Once you have become familiar with the possibilities of the machine, you can re-plan many recipes you regularly make. A little thought and imagination will provide endless ways in which a food processor can be of use when preparing major dishes.

Chicken and Barley
Casserole (page 69)

NAVARIN OF LAMB

Metric/Imperial	American
1 kg/2 lb middle neck of lamb cutlets	2 lb middle neck of lamb cutlets
15 g/½ oz butter or margarine	1 tablespoon butter or margarine
3 medium carrots, scraped	3 medium carrots, scraped
1 small white turnip, peeled and cut into thin slices	1 small white turnip, peeled and cut into thin slices
2 medium onions, peeled and quartered	2 medium onions, peeled and quartered
1 tablespoon flour	1 tablespoon flour
450 ml/¾ pint stock	2 cups stock
bouquet garni	bouquet garni
salt	salt
freshly ground black pepper	freshly ground black pepper

Trim the cutlets well. Melt the butter or margarine in a large frying pan (skillet) and brown meat on both sides. Remove and put into a casserole.

Fit the SLICING DISC and use to slice the carrots. Pack turnip into the feed tube and slice. (The turnip will slice into julienne strips.) Slice the onion. Sauté the carrots, turnip and onions in the frying pan (skillet) until just coloured. Stir in the flour and cook for 1 minute. Add the stock and bring to the boil. Pour over the meat. Add salt and pepper to taste and tuck in the bouquet garni. Cover and cook in a moderate oven (180°C/350°F, Gas Mark 4) for 1 to 1½ hours or until the meat is tender. This can also be cooked in a flameproof casserole, over a low heat.

Serves 4

LAMB AND ORANGE CASSEROLE

Metric/Imperial	American
2 onions, peeled	2 onions, peeled
2 sticks celery	2 sticks celery
1 tablespoon flour	1 tablespoon flour
salt	salt
freshly ground black pepper	freshly ground black pepper
750 g/1½ lb lean shoulder of lamb, cut into 4 cm/1½ inch pieces	1½ lb lean shoulder of lamb, cut into 1½ inch pieces
2 tablespoons vegetable oil	2 tablespoons vegetable oil
450 ml/¾ pint chicken stock	2 cups chicken stock
bouquet garni	bouquet garni
2 oranges	2 oranges
parsley, to garnish	parsley, to garnish

Fit the SLICING DISC. Slice the onions and celery and set aside. Mix the flour with salt and pepper, and toss the lamb in the seasoned flour.

Heat the oil in a frying pan (skillet) and fry the lamb until lightly coloured. Drain and put into a casserole. Add the onions and celery to the pan and cook gently for 5 minutes. Add any remaining seasoned flour, together with the stock, bouquet garni and more salt and pepper if necessary. Bring to the boil, stirring well, and pour over the lamb. Cover and cook in a moderate oven (160°C/325°F, Gas Mark 3) for 1 hour or until the lamb is tender. Remove bouquet garni.

While the lamb is cooking, prepare the oranges. Finely grate the rind of 1 orange. Thinly pare the rind from the other orange. Cut the rind into shreds and blanch. (To blanch: put the rind into cold water, bring to the boil and simmer for 2 minutes. Drain and refresh under cold running water.)

Remove all pith from the oranges and divide into segments. Stir the orange segments, with their juice, and the grated rind into the lamb and reheat carefully. Serve garnished with julienne strips of rind and parsley, chopped in the processor.

Serves 4

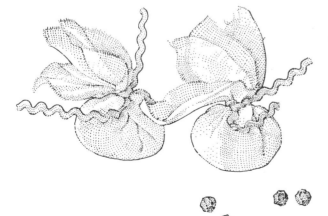

CHICKEN AND BARLEY CASSEROLE

Metric/Imperial	American
1 large onion, peeled and quartered	1 large onion, peeled and quartered
50 g/2 oz butter	¼ cup butter
225 g/8 oz firm button mushrooms	2 cups firm button mushrooms
225 g/8 oz pearl barley	1¼ cups pearl barley
750 ml/1¼ pints hot chicken stock	3 cups hot chicken stock
½ teaspoon powdered rosemary or 1 spray fresh rosemary	½ teaspoon powdered rosemary or 1 spray fresh rosemary
salt	salt
freshly ground black pepper	freshly ground black pepper
225 g/8 oz cold cooked chicken, diced	1 cup cold cooked diced chicken
chopped parsley	chopped parsley
grated Parmesan cheese	grated Parmesan cheese

Fit the METAL BLADE. Put the onion into the bowl and process until very finely chopped. Melt the butter in a large pan. Add the onion, stir over a low heat, then cover and allow to sweat.

Fit the SLICING DISC and use to slice the mushrooms. Add the barley and mushrooms to the onions. Toss to coat well with the butter, then cook for 3 to 4 minutes. Pour in the stock and rosemary (leave the spray whole and remove before serving) and add salt and pepper to taste. Mix in the chicken. Transfer to a casserole. Cover and bake in a moderate oven (180°C/350°F, Gas Mark 4) for about 1 hour or until the barley is tender. Sprinkle with the parsley and serve with grated Parmesan passed separately.

Serves 4

CHICKEN HASH MORNAY

Metric/Imperial	American
2 slices day-old white bread, crusts removed	2 slices day-old white bread, crusts removed
350–450 g/12 oz–1 lb cold, cooked chicken	1½–2 cups cold, cooked chicken
50 g/2 oz Cheddar cheese, roughly chopped	2 oz Cheddar cheese, roughly chopped
100 g/4 oz mushrooms, wiped	1 cup mushrooms, wiped
600 ml/1 pint hot cheese sauce	2½ cups hot cheese sauce

Fit the METAL BLADE. Tear the bread into pieces and place in the processor bowl. Process to fine crumbs. Remove and set aside. Put the cooked chicken in the bowl and using pulse action, roughly chop but do not over-process. Remove and set aside.

Fit the GRATING DISC and use to grate the cheese, set aside. Wash the bowl if necessary and fit the SLICING DISC. Slice the mushrooms and mix with the chicken. Stir the chicken mixture into hot cheese sauce and pour into a buttered oven or flameproof dish. Cover with the breadcrumbs and top with the grated cheese. Place in a hot oven (220°C/425°F, Gas Mark 7) or under a medium-hot grill (broiler) until heated through and crisp and brown on top.

Serves 4

PORK BALLS WITH PIQUANT SAUCE

Metric/Imperial	American
450 g/1 lb lean pork, cubed	1 lb lean pork, cubed
1 thick slice brown bread, crusts removed	1 thick slice brown bread, crusts removed
1 medium onion, peeled and quartered	1 medium onion, peeled and quartered
2 tablespoons of top of milk or single cream	2 tablespoons creamy milk or light cream
grated rind and juice of 1 lemon	grated rind and juice of 1 lemon
½ teaspoon each black peppercorns and coriander seeds, crushed	½ teaspoon each black peppercorns and coriander seeds, crushed
salt	salt
freshly ground black pepper	freshly ground black pepper
flour	flour
15 g/½ oz butter	1 tablespoon butter
1 tablespoon oil	1 tablespoon oil
3 medium leeks, well washed and trimmed	3 medium leeks, well washed and trimmed
1 × 400 g/14 oz can peeled tomatoes, drained and roughly chopped	1 × 14 oz can peeled tomatoes, drained and roughly chopped
3 tablespoons natural yogurt or single cream	3 tablespoons unflavored yogurt or light cream
chopped parsley	chopped parsley

Fit the METAL BLADE. Drop meat through feed tube into bowl, and mince (grind) finely. Remove meat and put into a large bowl. Break bread into pieces and process to fine crumbs. Add to the meat. Put onion into bowl and process until finely chopped. Add to meat in bowl together with milk or cream, lemon rind, peppercorns, coriander, salt and pepper. Stir to combine. Roll into 12 even-sized balls and coat with the flour. Shake off any excess.

In a frying pan (skillet), melt the butter and oil and brown the meatballs in batches; put in a casserole.

Fit the SLICING DISC and use to slice the leeks. Sauté the leeks in the fat remaining in the pan for about 5 minutes. Add the tomatoes and lemon juice and simmer over a medium heat, stirring, for about 5 minutes. Pour the sauce over the meatballs. Bake in a moderate oven (180°C/350°F, Gas Mark 4) for 20 to 30 minutes. Stir in the yogurt or cream just before serving. Sprinkle with the parsley.

Serves 4

NUTTY CHICKEN CROQUETTES

Metric/Imperial	American
4 slices fresh brown bread, crusts removed	4 slices brown bread, crusts removed
225 g/8 oz cold cooked chicken, cut into pieces	1 cup chopped cooked chicken
1 small onion, peeled and quartered	1 small onion, peeled and quartered
1 tablespoon parsley heads	1 tablespoon parsley heads
50 g/2 oz walnuts	½ cup walnuts
50 g/2 oz butter	¼ cup butter
50 g/2 oz flour	½ cup flour
250 ml/8 fl oz chicken stock	1 cup chicken stock
3 eggs	3 eggs
½ teaspoon chilli powder	½ teaspoon chili powder
salt	salt
freshly ground black pepper	freshly ground black pepper
oil or fat for deep-frying	oil or fat for deep-frying
TO GARNISH:	TO GARNISH:
lemon wedges	lemon wedges
parsley sprigs	parsley sprigs
TO SERVE:	TO SERVE:
spanish sauce (page 51)	spanish sauce (page 51)

Fit the METAL BLADE. Place the bread in the bowl and process to fine crumbs. Set aside. Put the chicken, onion and parsley heads into the bowl and process until finely minced (ground). Add walnuts and chop coarsely, using 3 bursts of pulse action. Remove and set aside.

Melt the butter in a pan and, when foaming, stir in the flour. Cook gently for 3 to 4 minutes, and gradually stir in the stock. Bring to the boil, stirring constantly. Reduce heat and continue cooking the 'panade' for 5 minutes. Beat in 2 of the eggs, the chicken mixture, chilli powder and salt and pepper. Spread on a cold plate and chill.

Beat the remaining egg and pour onto a plate. Mould the chicken mix into cork shapes on a floured surface. Dip into egg, then the reserved crumbs. Heat the oil or fat in a deep frying pan to 190°C/375°F. Slice the croquettes into the pan and cook until golden. Drain on kitchen paper. Arrange on a hot serving dish and garnish with lemon and parsley. Serve with Spanish Sauce.

Serves 4

Right: Pork Balls with Piquant Sauce and Nutty Chicken Croquettes

GALANTINE OF HAM

Metric/Imperial	American
2 large slices day-old bread, crusts removed	2 large slices day-old bread, crusts removed
1 medium onion, peeled and quartered	1 medium onion, peeled and quartered
25 g/1 oz butter or margarine	2 tablespoons butter or margarine
2 tomatoes, peeled, or 1 × 150 g/5 oz can tomatoes, drained	2 tomatoes, peeled or 1 × 5 oz can tomatoes, drained
450 g/1 lb cooked ham, or gammon, cut into 2.5 cm/1 inch cubes	1 lb cooked ham, cut into 1 inch cubes
4 bacon rashers, roughly cut up	4 slices Canadian bacon, roughly cut up
¼ teaspoon dried sage	¼ teaspoon dried sage
1 egg	1 egg
¼ teaspoon grated nutmeg	¼ teaspoon grated nutmeg
salt	salt
freshly ground black pepper	freshly ground black pepper

Fit the METAL BLADE. Break the bread into pieces, put in bowl and process to fine crumbs. Remove and place in a large bowl. Finely chop the onion, using pulse action.

Melt the butter or margarine in a frying pan (skillet). Add the onion and sauté for 5 minutes. Add the tomatoes and cook for another 5 minutes. Add to the breadcrumbs.

Finely mince (grind) the ham but do not process to a paste, add to the breadcrumbs. Mince the bacon using 3 or 4 bursts of pulse action. Add the bacon to the breadcrumbs with the sage, egg, nutmeg, salt and pepper. Mix thoroughly.

Grease a 1 kg/2 lb loaf tin (pan) or casserole and put in the mixture. Smooth the top and cover with foil. Bake in the centre of a moderately hot oven (190°C/375°F, Gas Mark 5) for 1½ hours. Allow to cool for a few minutes before serving hot. If serving cold, chill with a weight on top.

Serves 4 to 6

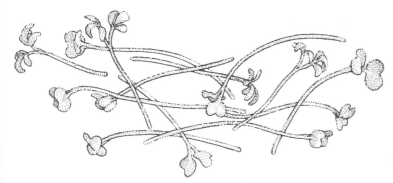

BACON AND EGG CUTLETS

Metric/Imperial	American
4 slices of bread, crusts removed	4 slices of bread, crusts removed
4 hard-boiled eggs, shelled and halved	4 hard-cooked eggs, shelled and halved
100 g/4 oz leftover cold boiled bacon, cut into pieces	½ cup chopped, cold leftover ham
salt	salt
freshly ground black pepper	freshly ground black pepper
25 g/1 oz butter	2 tablespoons butter
25 g/1 oz flour	¼ cup flour
150 ml/¼ pint milk	⅔ cup milk
1 egg, beaten	1 egg, beaten
oil for deep-frying	oil for deep-frying
few pieces uncooked macaroni	few pieces uncooked macaroni
TO GARNISH AND SERVE:	TO GARNISH AND SERVE:
mustard and cress	cress
sauté potatoes	sauté potatoes
grilled tomatoes	broiled tomatoes

Fit the METAL BLADE. Break the bread into pieces, place in the bowl and process to fine crumbs. Set aside. Put the eggs in the bowl and chop, using 3 or 4 bursts of pulse action. Set aside. Put the bacon into the bowl and process until finely chopped. Add to the eggs together with 50 g/2 oz of the crumbs and salt and pepper to taste.

Melt the butter in a pan and, when foaming, stir in the flour. Cook gently for 3 to 4 minutes. Gradually stir in the milk. Bring to the boil, stirring continuously, and simmer until the sauce is smooth and thick. Add the egg mixture and blend well. Adjust the seasoning and spread the mixture onto a plate. Leave to cool and firm.

Shape the mixture into 'cutlets' on a floured board. Dip into the beaten egg, then the remaining crumbs. Heat the oil or fat in a deep frying pan to 190°C/375°F. Gently lower the cutlets into the pan and cook until golden. Drain on kitchen paper. Stick a small piece of macaroni into the cutlet as the 'bone'. Serve on a hot dish, garnished with cress and accompanied by sauté potatoes and grilled (broiled) tomatoes.

Serves 4

CASSEROLED PORK AND VEGETABLES

Metric/Imperial	American
2 onions, peeled and quartered	2 onions, peeled and quartered
2 celery sticks	2 celery sticks
1 small green pepper, seeds removed	1 small green pepper, seeds removed
2 carrots, scraped	2 carrots, scraped
25 g/1 oz butter	2 tablespoons butter
2 tablespoons oil	2 tablespoons oil
25 g/1 oz plain flour	¼ cup all-purpose flour
salt	salt
freshly ground pepper	freshly ground pepper
750 g/1½ lb lean pork, cut into cubes	1½ lb lean pork, cut into cubes
600 ml/1 pint milk	2½ cups milk
1 bay leaf	1 bay leaf

Fit the METAL BLADE. Separately process the onions, celery and green pepper until chopped. Remove and set aside. Fit the SLICING DISC. Pack the carrots into the feed tube and slice. Remove.

Heat the butter and oil in a saucepan. Add the vegetables and cook gently until soft but not brown. Remove from the heat.

Mix the flour with salt and pepper to taste in a polythene (plastic) bag. Add the pork cubes and shake to coat with the flour. Add to the saucepan, in batches, and fry until browned on all sides. Stir in any remaining seasoned flour and cook, stirring, for 1 minute. Add the milk and bay leaf and bring to the boil. Cover and simmer for 1¼ to 1½ hours or until the pork is tender. Remove the bay leaf and serve hot.

Serves 4

BREAKFAST APPLEBURGERS

Metric/Imperial	American
2 eating apples, cored and quartered	2 eating apples, cored and quartered
2 slices fresh bread, crusts removed	2 slices fresh bread, crusts removed
225 g/8 oz pork sausage meat	½ lb pork sausage meat
1 egg, beaten	1 egg, beaten
salt	salt
freshly ground black pepper	freshly ground black pepper
TO GARNISH AND SERVE:	TO GARNISH AND SERVE:
4 streaky bacon rashers	4 slices fatty bacon
parsley sprigs	parsley sprigs
apple cream sauce (page 50)	apple cream sauce (page 50)

Fit the GRATING DISC. Grate the apples. Set aside and wipe out the bowl. Fit the METAL BLADE. Put the bread, broken into pieces, in the bowl and process to fine crumbs. Add the sausage meat, grated apple, egg and salt and pepper. Use 4 bursts of pulse action to combine the ingredients. Remove and shape into 4 burgers.

Trim the bacon and fry in a dry pan (skillet) until cooked but not hard. Roll up and keep hot. Fry the burgers in the bacon fat until cooked as liked. (Add a little butter if there is not sufficient fat.) Transfer burgers to a hot serving dish, top each one with a bacon roll and parsley sprig. Serve with apple cream sauce.

Serves 4

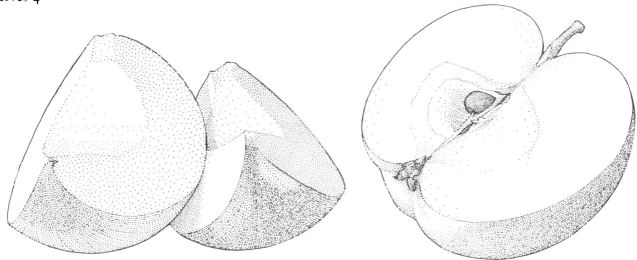

HUNGARIAN GOULASH

Metric/Imperial	American
750 g/1½ lb chuck or lean shin of beef, cut into 5 cm/2 inch cubes	1½ lb blade steak, cut into 2 inch cubes
2 tablespoons oil	2 tablespoons oil
1 large onion, peeled and quartered	1 large onion, peeled and quartered
1 clove garlic, crushed	1 clove garlic, crushed
1 tablespoon sweet Hungarian paprika	1 tablespoon sweet Hungarian paprika
1 tablespoon wholemeal flour	1 tablespoon wholewheat flour
1 tablespoon tomato purée	1 tablespoon tomato paste
450 ml/¾ pint beef stock, or 1 × 275 g/10½ oz can concentrated, undiluted consommé	¾ pint beef stock, or 1 × 10½ oz can concentrated, undiluted consommé
salt	salt
freshly ground black pepper	freshly ground black pepper
1 bay leaf	1 bay leaf
1 red pepper, seeded, or 1 whole cap canned red pimiento	1 red sweet pepper, seeded, or 1 whole cap canned red pimiento
175 g/6 oz tomatoes, peeled and quartered	¾ cup peeled and quartered tomatoes
150 ml/¼ pint soured cream	⅔ cup sour cream
noodles, dumplings or pumpernickel, to serve	noodles, dumplings or pumpernickel, to serve

Heat oil in a frying pan (skillet) and sear meat quickly on all sides. Remove with a slotted spoon and place in a casserole. Lower heat under pan (skillet). Fit the SLICING DISC and use to slice the onion. Sauté the onion and garlic in pan (skillet) for about 5 minutes. Add to casserole and mix with the meat. Stir paprika into pan (skillet), and cook gently for 2 minutes. Stir in flour, tomato purée (paste) and stock or consommé. Bring to the boil and add salt and pepper to taste.

Fit the METAL BLADE. Pour the stock mixture into the processor bowl, scraping the pan well, and process until smooth. Pour over the meat, and add the bay leaf. Cover with foil, then a lid and cook in a moderate oven (160°C/325°F, Gas Mark 3) for 2 hours or until meat is very tender. The goulash should not cook too rapidly. Remove from the oven.

Fit the SLICING DISC. Slice the red pepper or cut the pimiento into strips and stir into the goulash. Add the tomatoes and return the casserole to the oven to

Philadelphian Steak Tartare and Hungarian Goulash

reheat. Spoon over the cream at the last minute.

Serve with noodles or dumplings and, if possible, dark pumpernickel bread.

Serves 4 to 6

PHILADELPHIAN STEAK TARTARE

Metric/Imperial	American
225 g/8 oz fillet steak, tail end is ideal	½ lb boneless sirloin steak
2 tablespoons parsley heads	2 tablespoons parsley heads
1 egg yolk	1 egg yolk
1 small onion, peeled and quartered	1 small onion, peeled and quartered
2 anchovy fillets	2 anchovy fillets
1 tablespoon lemon juice	1 tablespoon lemon juice
1 tablespoon Dijon mustard	1 tablespoon Dijon mustard
1 tablespoon capers	1 tablespoon capers
1 teaspoon Worcestershire sauce	1 teaspoon Worcestershire sauce
few drops Tabasco sauce	few drops Tabasco sauce
salt	salt
freshly ground black pepper	freshly ground black pepper
dark rye bread, to serve	dark rye bread, to serve
parsley, to garnish	parsley, to garnish

Trim the meat carefully, removing all skin and gristle and cut into eight pieces.

Fit the METAL BLADE. Place all the ingredients, except the bread and parsley, into the bowl and process until finely minced (ground), almost a purée (paste). Check the seasoning. Serve chilled, spread on slices of dark rye bread and dusted with parsley, which has been chopped in the processor.

Serves 4

BEEF HASH PIE

Metric/Imperial	American
75 g/3 oz Cheddar cheese, cut into pieces	3 oz Cheddar cheese, cut into pieces
1 large onion, peeled and quartered	1 large onion, peeled and quartered
25 g/1 oz butter	2 tablespoons butter
100 g/4 oz cold cooked carrot	¼ lb cold cooked carrot
225 g/8 oz cold cooked potato (not mashed)	½ lb cold cooked potato (not mashed)
75 g/3 oz pickled beetroot	3 oz pickled beets
1 egg	1 egg
1 tablespoon parsley heads, chopped	1 tablespoon parsley heads, chopped
350 g/12 oz corned beef, cut into pieces	¾ lb corned beef, cut into pieces
2 tablespoons red wine or leftover gravy	2 tablespoons red wine or leftover gravy
salt	salt
freshly ground black pepper	freshly ground black pepper
parsley, to garnish	parsley, to garnish

Fit the GRATING DISC and use to grate the cheese. Set aside. Grate the onion. Melt the butter in a small pan and add the onion. Cook gently until soft. Meanwhile, grate the carrot, potato and beetroot (beet) and reserve.

Fit the PLASTIC BLADE. Put all the ingredients, except the cheese and parsley to garnish, into the bowl. Process until the meat is roughly chopped and the egg is blended. Turn into a pie dish. Sprinkle with the cheese and bake in a moderately hot oven (190°C/375°F, Gas Mark 5) for 30 minutes or until golden and bubbling and heated through. Sprinkle with parsley, chopped in the processor, and serve with Savoury French Stick (page 64).

Serves 4

BEEF STROGANOFF

Metric/Imperial	American
1 kg/2 lb rump steak	2 lb boneless sirloin steak
5 tablespoons plain flour	5 tablespoons all-purpose flour
salt	salt
450 g/1 lb onions, peeled and quartered	1 lb onions, peeled and quartered
450 g/1 lb small mushrooms, stalks removed	1 lb small mushrooms, stalks removed
100 g/4 oz butter	½ cup butter
1 tablespoon tomato purée	1 tablespoon tomato paste
1 tablespoon Worcestershire sauce	1 tablespoon Worcestershire sauce
freshly ground black pepper	freshly ground black pepper
2 tablespoons dry sherry	2 tablespoons dry sherry
300 ml/½ pint soured cream	1¼ cups sour cream

Trim the meat and cut into thin slices. Season 3 tablespoons of the flour with salt to taste and toss with the meat to coat. Shake off any excess flour from the meat.

Fit the METAL BLADE. Process the onions, in batches, until finely chopped. Remove and set aside.

Fit the SLICING DISC. Put the mushrooms into the feed tube and slice. Remove and set aside.

Melt 75 g/3 oz/6 tablespoons of the butter and add the onions. Cook until just coloured, about 10 minutes. Add the mushrooms and cook for a few more minutes. Remove the onions and mushrooms and set aside. Add the beef strips to the pan and fry briskly for 3 to 4 minutes, adding the remaining butter when necessary. Return the onions and mushrooms to the pan with plenty of salt and pepper. Shake all well together and cook over a low heat for 1 minute. Add the tomato purée (paste), Worcestershire sauce, sherry and soured cream.

Cook for a few minutes longer or until heated through. If the mixture is a little dry add some beef stock.

Serve immediately with cooked noodles.

Serves 8

MEAT LOAF

Metric/Imperial	American
small bunch parsley, washed and dried	small bunch of parsley, washed and dried
2 slices slightly stale bread, crusts removed and broken into pieces	2 slices slightly stale bread, crusts removed and broken into pieces
225 g/8 oz pie veal, trimmed	1 cup (½ lb) pie veal, trimmed
450 g/1 lb lean beef, cubed	2 cups (1 lb) cubed lean beef
225 g/8 oz lean pork, cubed	1 cup (½ lb) cubed lean pork
1 medium onion, peeled and quartered	1 medium onion, peeled and quartered
25 g/1 oz lard	2 tablespoons shortening
1 large clove garlic, crushed	1 large clove garlic, crushed
1½ teaspoons salt	1½ teaspoons salt
½ teaspoon freshly ground black pepper	½ teaspoon freshly ground black pepper
¼ teaspoon ground allspice	¼ teaspoon ground allspice
1 teaspoon dried thyme	1 teaspoon dried thyme
1 bay leaf	1 bay leaf
3 rashers streaky bacon	3 slices fatty bacon

Fit the METAL BLADE. Put the parsley in the bowl and process until very finely chopped. Remove and place in a mixing bowl. Process the bread to coarse breadcrumbs and place in the bowl. Process the meats separately until minced (ground) to a medium-fine texture. Add to the parsley. Process the onion until finely chopped.

Melt the lard (shortening) in a frying pan (skillet) and sauté the onion and garlic until just translucent. Add to the parsley with the salt, pepper, allspice and thyme. Mix with your hands, working the mixture until it is well blended. Pack into a greased 1 kg/2 lb loaf tin (pan) and place the bay leaf on top. Stretch the bacon rashers with the back of a knife and lay them lengthwise on the meat loaf. Bake in the centre of a moderate oven (180°C/350°F, Gas Mark 4) for 1½ hours. Stand the loaf tin (pan) in a warm place for 30 minutes before slicing.

To serve cold, cover with foil, cover with another loaf tin (pan) into which are placed heavy objects. Cool and refrigerate overnight.

Serves 5 to 6

HAMBURGERS HOLSTEIN

Metric/Imperial	American
1 bunch spring onions	1 bunch scallions
1 kg/2 lb lean beef, cut into 2.5 cm/1 inch cubes	2 lb lean beef, cut into 1 inch cubes
25 g/1 oz butter or margarine, softened	2 tablespoons butter or margarine, softened
salt	salt
freshly ground black pepper	freshly ground black pepper
½ teaspoon dried marjoram	½ teaspoon dried marjoram
½ teaspoon dried thyme	½ teaspoon dried thyme
½ teaspoon dried basil	½ teaspoon dried basil
4 eggs, poached	4 eggs, poached

Fit the METAL BLADE. Using pulse action, chop the spring onions (scallions) finely. Remove and place in a large bowl. Make sure the meat is well trimmed of gristle and tendons. Drop meat through the feed tube and process until minced (ground). Check texture by stopping motor, waiting until blade no longer whirls, and removing a piece of meat with plastic spatula or wooden spoon. The texture should be fairly fine. Mix the meat, onions (scallions), butter or margarine, salt, pepper, and herbs. Shape the mixture into four burgers.

Grill (broil) the burgers, or cook them in a non-stick frying pan (skillet), until rare, medium or well done, according to taste. Top with hot poached eggs.

This is a good plain supper dish served with mashed potatoes and a salad.

Serves 4

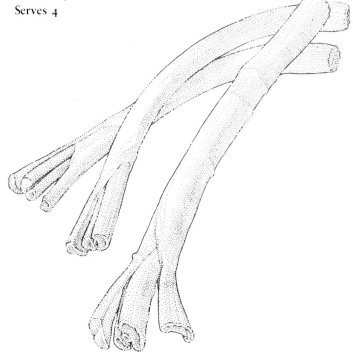

SHRIMP CURRY

Metric/Imperial	American
1 large stick celery, trimmed and cut into tube-size pieces	1 large stick celery, trimmed and cut into tube-size pieces
1 × 225 g/8 oz can water chestnuts, drained	1 × 8 oz can water chestnuts drained
1 small onion, peeled and halved	1 small onion, peeled and halved
½ green pepper, seeded	½ green pepper, seeded
1 large cooking apple, cored and quartered	1 large baking apple, cored and quartered
1 clove garlic, crushed	1 clove garlic, crushed
4 tablespoons groundnut oil	¼ cup peanut oil
2 tablespoons curry powder, or to taste	2 tablespoons curry powder, or to taste
½ teaspoon ground ginger	½ teaspoon ground ginger
450 g/1 lb fresh or frozen shrimps or prawns, shelled and defrosted	2 cups peeled fresh or frozen defrosted shrimps
2 tablespoons sherry	2 tablespoons sherry
1 × 280 g/10½ oz can concentrated cream of mushroom soup	1 × 10½ oz can concentrated cream of mushroom soup

Baked Fish with Olives,
Arbroath Hot Pot and
Shrimp Curry

Fit the SLICING DISC and use to slice the celery and water chestnuts. Remove both and put into a bowl. Fit the METAL BLADE. Put the onion in the bowl and coarsely chop, using pulse action. Add to the celery. Chop the green pepper and apple coarsely using pulse action. Add to the celery with the garlic.

In a large frying pan (skillet) heat the oil and sauté the vegetable mixture until nearly cooked but still crisp. Stir in the curry powder and ginger and cook for about 2 minutes, stirring all the time. Add the shrimps, sherry, soup and enough water to thin to the desired consistency. Bring to a boil then simmer for a further 5 minutes until heated through and well blended. The vegetables and apple should be slightly crisp and not limp.

Serve with mango chutney and steamed rice, or any other accompaniments you like, such as poppadums.
Serves 6

ARBROATH HOT POT

Metric/Imperial	American
25 g/1 oz brown or rye bread, crusts removed	1 oz brown or rye bread, crusts removed
450 g/1 lb potatoes, peeled	1 lb potatoes, peeled
2 onions, peeled	2 onions, peeled
3 Arbroath smokies, skinned and filleted	3 bucklings, skinned and filleted
salt if required	salt if required
freshly ground black pepper	freshly ground black pepper
2 eggs	2 eggs
300 ml/½ pint milk, or enough to barely cover	1¼ cups milk, or enough to barely cover
25 g/1 oz butter	2 tablespoons butter
TO GARNISH AND SERVE:	TO GARNISH AND SERVE:
lemon butterflies (optional)	lemon butterflies (optional)
parsley sprigs (optional)	parsley sprigs (optional)
buttered almond sauce (page 50)	buttered almond sauce (page 50)

Fit the METAL BLADE. Break the bread into pieces and process to fine crumbs. Set aside. Fit the SLICING DISC and use to slice the potatoes. Set aside. Slice the onions and set aside.

Butter a 750 ml/1¼ pint/3¾ cup ovenproof dish and dust with the crumbs. Make layers of the potatoes, onions and fish, seasoning the layers with pepper. (Salt may not be necessary if the fish is salty.) Finish with a layer of potatoes, arranged in a circle. Beat the eggs and milk with a little pepper and pour over the potatoes. Dot the butter over the top. Bake in a moderate oven (180°C/350°F, Gas Mark 4) for 30 minutes. Reduce the heat to 160°C/325°F, Gas Mark 3 and bake for a further 30 minutes or until the potatoes are tender. Serve hot, garnished with lemon and parsley and accompanied by Buttered Almond Sauce.

Serves 4

BAKED FISH WITH OLIVES

Metric/Imperial	American
1 onion, peeled and halved	1 onion, peeled and halved
25 stuffed olives	25 stuffed olives
1 large red pepper, seeded and quartered	1 large red pepper, seeded and quartered
5 tablespoons fresh coriander or 2 teaspoons dried	5 tablespoons fresh coriander or 2 teaspoons dried
1 tablespoon oil	1 tablespoon oil
90 ml/3 fl oz orange juice	⅓ cup orange juice
3 tablespoons lemon juice	3 tablespoons lemon juice
salt	salt
freshly ground black pepper	freshly ground black pepper
2 kg/4 lb whole red mullet	4 lb whole red mullet
butter for greasing	butter for greasing

Fit the METAL BLADE. Process the onion until roughly chopped. Remove and set aside. Process the olives, pepper and fresh coriander until roughly chopped. Remove and set aside.

Heat the oil in a frying pan (skillet) and cook the onion until soft and transparent. Add the olive mixture and cook for a few minutes, stirring. Add the orange and lemon juices, dried coriander, if using, and salt and pepper to taste. Grease a shallow ovenproof dish that is large enough to take the fish. Season the fish generously with salt and pepper and place in the dish. Pour over the sauce.

Bake uncovered in a moderately hot oven (200°C/400°F, Gas Mark 6) for about 40 to 60 minutes, or until cooked when tested, basting every 10 minutes.

Serve with boiled potatoes and vegetables in season. Other fish may be used.

Serves 6 to 8

VEGETARIAN PEANUT LOAF

Metric/Imperial	American
150 ml/¼ pint vegetable stock	⅔ cup vegetable stock
50 g/2 oz medium oatmeal	⅓ cup medium oatmeal
100 g/4 oz Cheddar cheese	¼ lb Cheddar cheese
50 g/2 oz slice fresh wholemeal bread, crusts removed and broken into pieces	2 oz slice fresh wholewheat bread, crusts removed and broken into pieces
175 g/6 oz salted peanuts	1 cup salted peanuts
1 onion, peeled and quartered	1 onion, peeled and quartered
2 teaspoons lemon juice	2 teaspoons lemon juice
1 egg, beaten	1 egg, beaten
50 g/2 oz peanut butter, softened in a little milk	¼ cup peanut butter, softened in a little milk
freshly ground black pepper	freshly ground black pepper
small can condensed mushroom soup or cranberry sauce, to serve	small can condensed mushroom soup or cranberry sauce, to serve

Bring the stock to a boil and sprinkle on the oats, stirring constantly. Bring back to the boil, cover and simmer over a very gentle heat for 10 minutes. Pour into a mixing bowl.

Fit the GRATING DISC and use to grate the cheese, add to the mixing bowl. Fit the METAL BLADE and process the bread to fine crumbs. Tip into the mixing bowl. Process the peanuts until finely chopped and add to the mixing bowl. Finally process onion until chopped, add to bowl and mix all ingredients well. Taste and adjust seasoning. Grease a 450 g/1 lb loaf tin (pan) and fill with the mixture. Bake in a moderate oven (180°C/350°F, Gas Mark 4) for about 1 hour. Turn onto a heated dish.

A small tin of condensed mushroom soup makes a good sauce. Cranberry sauce also goes well with this recipe.

Serves 4

COURGETTE (ZUCCHINI) PANCAKES

Metric/Imperial	American
1½ teaspoons fresh mint leaves or ¾ teaspoon dried	1½ teaspoons fresh mint leaves or ¾ teaspoon dried
3 medium courgettes	3 medium zucchini
1 teaspoon salt	1 teaspoon salt
225 g/8 oz feta cheese, drained	½ lb feta cheese, drained
freshly ground pepper	freshly ground pepper
3 eggs	3 eggs
3 tablespoons plain flour	3 tablespoons all-purpose flour
butter for frying	butter for frying

Fit the METAL BLADE. Process the mint until finely chopped. Remove and set aside. Fit the GRATING DISC.

Top and tail the courgettes (zucchini), pack into the feed tube and grate. Remove, place on a plate and sprinkle with the salt. Put another plate on the courgettes (zucchini), add a weight and leave for an hour. Drain off any liquid.

Put the cheese in the feed tube and grate. Combine the cheese, mint and courgette (zucchini) with pepper to taste.

Fit the PLASTIC BLADE. Put the eggs in the bowl and use 2 or 3 bursts of pulse action to combine. Add the eggs to the cheese mixture and stir until combined.

Heat some butter in a frying pan (skillet) and fry spoonfuls of the mixture until crisp and golden on both sides, turning when necessary. Drain on kitchen paper.

Serve with Savoury French Stick (page 64) and any of the salads.

Serves 4

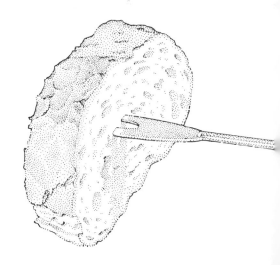

ZERMATT FONDUE

Metric/Imperial	American
225 g/8 oz Emmenthal cheese, roughly chopped	½ lb Emmenthal cheese, roughly chopped
225 g/8 oz Gruyère cheese, roughly chopped	½ lb Gruyère cheese, roughly chopped
300 ml/½ pint dry white wine	1¼ cups dry white wine
1 tablespoon cornflour	1 tablespoon cornstarch
1 small clove garlic, crushed	1 small clove garlic, crushed
salt	salt
freshly ground black pepper	freshly ground black pepper
1 tablespoon Kirsch (optional)	1 tablespoon Kirsch (optional)
TO SERVE:	TO SERVE:
French bread	French bread

Fit the GRATING DISC. Drop cheeses through the feed tube, grate and put into a heavy saucepan. Reserve 3 tablespoons of the wine and bring the rest to just below boiling. Pour onto the cheese, cover, and cook slowly until the cheese melts. Fit the METAL BLADE.

Just before serving, blend the cornflour (cornstarch) with the reserved wine and stir into the cheese mixture. Pour the cheese and wine mixture into the processor bowl and using pulse action, blend briefly until smooth. Pour into a fondue pot and stir in the garlic, salt, pepper, and Kirsch if used.

Serve hot with chunks of French bread speared on forks.

Serves 4 to 6

CHICK PEA CASSEROLE

Metric/Imperial	American
225 g/8 oz dried chick peas, soaked overnight	1 cup dried chick peas, soaked overnight
225 g/8 oz cabbage, cored	½ lb cabbage, cored
1 onion, peeled and quartered	1 onion, peeled and quartered
1 green pepper, seeds removed	1 green pepper, seeds removed
450 g/1 lb tomatoes, peeled	1 lb tomatoes, peeled
½ teaspoon ground ginger	½ teaspoon ground ginger
pinch ground cloves	pinch ground cloves
salt	salt
freshly ground pepper	freshly ground pepper

Drain the chick peas, cover with fresh water and bring to the boil. Cover and simmer for 2 hours or until tender, adding more boiling water if necessary. Drain, reserving the liquid.

Fit the GRATING DISC. Cut the cabbage into tube-size pieces, put into the feed tube and grate. Remove and set aside.

Fit the METAL BLADE. Process the onion until roughly chopped. Remove and set aside. Process the green pepper until diced, remove and set aside. Process the tomatoes until chopped, remove and set aside.

Heat the oil in a large frying pan (skillet). Add the onion and fry until it is soft but not brown. Add the tomatoes, cabbage and green pepper and fry for a further 5 minutes. Add the ginger, cloves, salt and pepper to taste. Stir in the drained chick peas.

Turn the mixture into a casserole and stir in 300 ml/½ pint/1¼ cups of the reserved chick pea cooking liquid. Cover and cook in a moderate oven (180°C/350°F, Gas Mark 4) for 1 hour. Serve hot from the casserole.

Serves 4

DESSERTS

What is it about sweet things that makes us think of them as treats? A certain forbidden delight or the threat of calories and tooth decay lurking in every mouthful.

Whatever the reason, there are very few people (especially men) whose mouth doesn't water at the thought of a dessert. Whether serving a luscious dessert such as Chocolate Profiteroles or a simpler Dutch Banana Cream (see pages 100 and 93), a food processor will quickly and easily prepare all these desserts and many more.

A food processor is excellent for preparing a pancake (crêpe) batter from which Serniki (page 84) can be made or combining the ingredients for a cheesecake (page 86). Ice creams are also successful in a processor, where the blending of egg yolks and sugar takes place and the partially frozen mixture is beaten to improve the texture. Small children particularly benefit from a processor, as fruit purées can be quickly prepared if the rest of the family are having a dessert the children don't like. Fruit salads are particularly successful as the fruit can be prepared at the last minute. Simply pour a sugar syrup over the prepared fruit and the salad is ready.

The great advantage of a food processor is the speed with which it can prepare desserts at the last minute with no fuss or bother.

Rich Treacle (Syrup) Tart
(page 85)

PANCAKES (CRÊPES)

Metric/Imperial	American
100 g/4 oz plain flour	1 cup plain flour
pinch of salt	pinch of salt
300 ml/½ pint milk	1¼ cups milk
1 egg	1 egg
15 g/½ oz butter, melted	1 tablespoon butter, melted

Fit the PLASTIC BLADE. Put the flour and salt into the bowl. With the machine turned on, add the milk and egg and process until blended, using 2 or 3 bursts of pulse action. Add the melted butter and blend. Pour the mixture into a measuring jug and leave to rest for 30 minutes.

Heat a heavy 15 cm (6 inch) frying pan (skillet) and grease lightly with oil or butter. Pour sufficient batter over the base of the pan to coat tilting the pan so all holes are covered. Cook until slightly golden underneath then turn and cook the other side. Remove and repeat with the remaining batter.

Stack the pancakes (crêpes) on a plate, separated by pieces of greaseproof (wax) paper. The pancakes (crêpes) will keep for up to a week in the refrigerator or can be frozen.

Makes 12 pancakes (crêpes)

SERNIKI

Metric/Imperial	American
225 g/8 oz cottage cheese	1 cup cottage cheese
50 g/2 oz caster sugar	¼ cup sugar
1 egg yolk	1 egg yolk
75 g/3 oz butter	¼ cup plus 2 tablespoons butter
50 g/2 oz sultanas	⅓ cup seedless white raisins
2 teaspoons orange flower water	2 teaspoons orange flower water
8 pancakes (above)	8 crêpes (above)
sifted icing sugar, to decorate	sifted confectioners' sugar, to decorate
fresh orange segments, to serve (optional)	fresh orange segments, to serve (optional)

Fit the PLASTIC BLADE. Put the cottage cheese, sugar, egg yolk and 50 g/2 oz/¼ cup of the butter in the bowl and process until smooth. Place in a bowl and stir in the sultanas (seedless white raisins) and orange flower water. Divide the mixture equally between the pancakes (crêpes). Roll up, turning in the sides to completely enclose the filling.

Melt the remaining butter in a frying pan (skillet) and place the pancakes (crêpes) side and side. Cook gently on each side until golden. Serve hot, sprinkled with sifted icing (confectioners') sugar. Fresh orange segments are delicious served with Serniki.

Serves 4

ORANGE AND WALNUT PANCAKES (CRÊPES)

Metric/Imperial	American
100 g/4 oz walnuts	1 cup walnuts
175 g/6 oz cream cheese	¾ cup cream cheese
2 tablespoons lemon juice	2 tablespoons lemon juice
175 g/6 oz orange marmalade	½ cup orange marmalade
12 cooked pancakes (left)	12 cooked crêpes (left)
50 g/2 oz butter	¼ cup butter
2 tablespoons Grand Marnier (optional)	2 tablespoons Grand Marnier (optional)
2 whole oranges, to decorate	2 whole oranges, to decorate

Fit the METAL BLADE and use to coarsely chop the walnuts. Set aside. Fit the plastic blade. Put the cream cheese and lemon juice in the bowl. Process, using 3 or 4 bursts of pulse action, until smooth. Combine the marmalade and nuts. Make the pancakes (crêpes) as described on the left.

Spread each pancake (crêpe) with the cheese mixture, leaving a border. Cover each with the marmalade mixture, dividing it evenly, and fold into quarters.

Melt the butter in a large frying pan (skillet). Sauté the pancakes (crêpes) on each side until heated through. Transfer to a heated serving dish and sprinkle with the Grand Marnier, if used. Remove every shred of peel, pith and membrane from the oranges and segment them. Decorate the pancakes (crêpes) with the orange segments.

Serves 6

CHESTNUT PANCAKES (CRÊPES)

Metric/Imperial	American
1 tablespoon strong black liquid coffee	*1 tablespoon strong black liquid coffee*
2 tablespoons rum or brandy	*2 tablespoons rum or brandy*
1 × 225 g/8 oz can sweetened chestnut purée	*1 × ½ lb can sweetened chestnut purée*
300 ml/½ pint double cream	*1¼ cups heavy cream*
12 pancakes (far left)	*12 crêpes (far left)*
icing sugar, to finish	*confectioners' sugar, to finish*

Fit the PLASTIC BLADE. Put the coffee, 1 tablespoon of the rum or brandy and the chestnut purée in the processor bowl. Using a pulse action, combine the ingredients. Turn into a bowl.

Lightly whip the cream and fold half into the chestnut mixture. Spread the chestnut mixture evenly over the pancakes (crêpes) and roll up into cigar shapes. Arrange on a serving dish and spoon over the remaining cream, flavoured with the remaining rum or brandy. Dredge with a little icing (confectioners') sugar before serving.

Serves 4 to 6

RICH TREACLE (SYRUP) TART

Metric/Imperial	American
75 g/3 oz crustless bread or plain cake, broken into pieces	*3 oz crustless bread or plain cake, broken into pieces*
225 g/8 oz golden syrup	*1 cup corn syrup*
1 egg, beaten	*1 egg, beaten*
grated rind and juice of ½ lemon	*grated rind and juice of ½ lemon*
225 g/8 oz sweet shortcrust pastry (page 101)	*½ lb sweet basic pie dough (page 101)*

Fit the METAL BLADE. Put the bread or cake into the processor bowl and process to fine crumbs. Set aside.

Mix together the syrup, egg, lemon rind and juice. Stir in the crumbs. Roll out the pastry and use to line a 20 cm/8 inch flan tin (pie tin). Fill with the syrup mixture. Bake in a moderately hot oven (200°C/400°F, Gas Mark 6) for 10 minutes. Reduce the heat to 180°C/350°F, Gas Mark 4 and bake for a further 20 minutes. Allow to cool and the filling will set. This is at its best, when served warm. Serve with pouring cream.

Serves 4 to 6

ITALIAN CHEESECAKE

Metric/Imperial	American
225 g/8 oz digestive biscuits	½ lb Graham crackers
100 g/4 oz butter or margarine, melted	½ cup butter or margarine, melted
2 eggs, separated	2 eggs, separated
225 g/8 oz curd cheese	½ lb cream cheese
grated rind and juice of 1 lemon	grated rind and juice of 1 lemon
175 ml/6 fl oz double cream	¾ cup heavy cream
75 g/3 oz caster sugar	⅓ cup sugar
2 tablespoons gelatine	2 tablespoons unflavored gelatin
5 tablespoons boiling water	5 tablespoons boiling water
50 g/2 oz sultanas or raisins	⅓ cup seedless white raisins or raisins

Fit the METAL BLADE. Using pulse action, process the biscuits (crackers) to medium crumbs. Remove and mix with the butter or margarine. Press into the base of a loose-bottomed cake tin (springform pan), 18 cm/7 inch in diameter and 9 cm/3½ inch high.

Fit the PLASTIC BLADE. Place the egg yolks, curd (cream) cheese, lemon rind and juice, cream and sugar into the processor bowl. Process to blend for about 30 seconds, scraping down when necessary.

Dissolve the gelatine in boiling water, allow to cool slightly, then pour through feed tube onto mixture. Using pulse action, blend in 2 or 3 bursts.

Whisk the egg whites until stiff but not dry. Add sultanas (seedless white raisins) or raisins to processor mixture and stir in with plastic spatula. Tip contents of processor bowl onto the egg whites and cut through, lightly, with a metal spoon, taking care not to beat out the air. Pour onto crumb base and chill for 3 to 4 hours. Serve in small slices.
Makes 10 small portions

water until the mixture begins to thicken. Remove from the saucepan and cool.

Whisk the double (heavy) cream to soft peak stage and fold into custard mixture. Pour into a suitable freezer container and freeze until half frozen. Turn into a chilled bowl and beat to break down the ice crystals. (This helps give a smooth texture.) Return to the freezer until frozen then cover and leave until ready to serve.

Take the ice cream out of the freezer and put in the main part of refrigerator about 30 minutes before serving. This makes the ice cream softer to serve and the flavour is better.

Serves 6 to 8

MOCHA ICE CREAM

Metric/Imperial	American
100 g/4 oz plain chocolate, broken into pieces	4 squares semi-sweet chocolate, broken into pieces
4 tablespoons hot strong coffee	$\frac{1}{4}$ cup hot strong coffee
4 egg yolks	4 egg yolks
50 g/2 oz sugar	$\frac{1}{4}$ cup sugar
300 ml/$\frac{1}{2}$ pint milk	$1\frac{1}{4}$ cups milk
150 ml/$\frac{1}{4}$ pint double cream	$\frac{2}{3}$ cup heavy cream
2 egg whites	2 egg whites

Fit the GRATING DISC and use to grate the chocolate. Place in a small bowl and pour the hot coffee over. Stir to melt the chocolate.

Fit the METAL BLADE. Put the egg yolks and sugar into the processor bowl and process until thick and pale. Heat the milk until nearly boiling. Slowly pour through the feed tube and blend. Pour in the melted chocolate mixture and process to blend. Scrape out into a heatproof bowl and set over a pan of simmering water. Cook, stirring until the mixture just begins to thicken. Cool.

Whisk the cream lightly and fold into the custard mixture. Whisk the egg whites until stiff peaks form and fold into the mixture with a metal spoon. Pour into a suitable freezer container and freeze. Cover and leave until ready to serve. Put into the main part of the refrigerator about 30 minutes before serving.

This ice cream does not need beating and refreezing as most ices do.

Serves 6

SUPER VANILLA ICE CREAM

Metric/Imperial	American
4 egg yolks	4 egg yolks
100 g/4 oz caster sugar	$\frac{1}{2}$ cup sugar
300 ml/$\frac{1}{2}$ pint single cream	$1\frac{1}{4}$ cups light cream
$\frac{1}{2}$ teaspoon vanilla essence	$\frac{1}{2}$ teaspoon vanilla extract
300 ml/$\frac{1}{2}$ pint double cream	$1\frac{1}{4}$ cups heavy cream

Fit the PLASTIC BLADE. Blend the egg yolks and sugar until thick and pale. Heat the single (light) cream with the vanilla essence (extract) until just below boiling point. Pour slowly through the feed tube with the machine switched on and blend for 10 seconds. Scrape the mixture into a heatproof bowl that will fit over a saucepan of simmering water (do not let base of bowl touch water). Cook, stirring, over simmering

Italian Cheesecake, Super Vanilla Ice Cream served with Chocolate Brandy Sauce (page 55) and Mocha Ice Cream

VANILLA AND LEMON CHEESECAKE

Metric/Imperial	American
250 ml/8 fl oz natural yogurt	1 cup unflavored yogurt
grated rind of ½ a lemon	grated rind of ½ a lemon
225 g/8 oz caster sugar	1 cup sugar
750 g/1½ lb low fat cottage cheese, sieved	3 cups low fat cottage cheese, sieved
5 eggs	5 eggs
3 tablespoons plain flour	3 tablespoons all-purpose flour
vanilla essence to taste	vanilla extract to taste
praline, to decorate	praline, to decorate

Put the yogurt in a large mixing bowl and stir in the sugar and lemon rind. Fit the PLASTIC BLADE. Place the cottage cheese, eggs, flour and vanilla in the processor bowl and process for about 10 seconds. Add the yogurt mixture and process for 2 seconds.

Grease a 23 cm/9 inch square cake tin (pan) and pour in the mixture. Bake in a moderate oven (180°C/350°F, Gas Mark 4) for about 40 minutes or until the cheesecake begins to shrink from the sides of the tin (pan). Chill. Decorate with crushed praline.
Serves 8

ORANGE LIQUEUR ICE CREAM

Metric/Imperial	American
2 thin-skinned juicy oranges, roughly cut up	2 thin-skinned juicy oranges, roughly cut up
6 egg yolks	6 egg yolks
225 g/8 oz caster sugar	1 cup sugar
2 tablespoons Curaçao	2 tablespoons Curaçao
300 ml/½ pint double cream	1¼ cups heavy cream

Fit the METAL BLADE. Feed the oranges through the feed tube, and process until pulped. Remove.

Fit the PLASTIC BLADE. Blend the egg yolks and sugar until pale and thick. Add the pulped oranges and liqueur and blend for 10 seconds. Scrape into a bowl.

Whisk the cream lightly but do not let it become too stiff. Using a metal spoon fold it through the orange mixture. Pour into a suitable freezer container and freeze. Cover and leave until ready to use. Soften in the refrigerator for 30 minutes before serving.
Serves 6 to 8

Variation

Whisk two of the egg whites until foamy. Add two tablespoons of caster sugar and continue whisking until the mixture hold stiff peaks. Fold in to the orange mixture after the cream. This makes a lighter ice cream.

CHESTNUT ICE CREAM

Metric/Imperial	American
3 egg yolks	3 egg yolks
50 g/2 oz caster sugar	¼ cup sugar
250 ml/8 fl oz milk, scalded and cooled	1 cup milk, scalded and cooled
1 × 200 g/7 oz can sweetened chestnut purée	1 × 7 oz can sweetened chestnut paste
120 ml/4 fl oz double cream	½ cup heavy cream
TO SERVE:	TO SERVE:
chocolate sauce	chocolate sauce
marron glacé	candied chestnut

Fit the METAL BLADE. Put the yolks and sugar into the bowl and process using pulse action until thick and light. Pour in the milk through the feed tube and blend, using 2 bursts of pulse action. Pour the mixture into a saucepan and stir over a gentle heat until the custard thickens but do not allow to boil. Pour into a clean bowl and leave to cool completely. Cover with greaseproof (wax) paper, on the surface.

Stir in the chestnut purée (paste) and cream. Pour into a suitable freezer container and freeze until very thick but not completely solid. Scrape into the processor bowl and process until smooth. Pour into a container, cover and freeze. Serve with chocolate sauce and sliced marron glacé (candied chestnut).
Serves 4 to 6

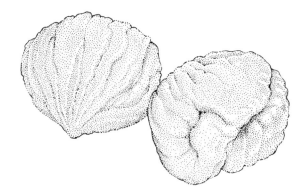

FRENCH PLUM PUDDING

Metric/Imperial	American
750 g/1½ lb ripe plums, stoned	1½ lb ripe plums, pitted
100 g/4 oz caster sugar	½ cup sugar
75 g/3 oz plain flour	¾ cup all-purpose flour
3 eggs	3 eggs
450 ml/¾ pint milk	2 cups milk
½ teaspoon almond essence	½ teaspoon almond extract
40 g/1½ oz butter	3 tablespoons butter
sugar to serve	sugar to serve

Butter a shallow ovenproof dish, put in the fruit and dust with 2 tablespoons of the sugar.

Fit the PLASTIC BLADE. Put the flour, eggs, milk and essence (extract) into the processor bowl and process until smooth. Add the remaining sugar and process for 10 seconds. Pour the batter over the fruit and flake the remaining butter on top. Bake in the centre of a hot oven (220°C/400°F, Gas Mark 7) for about 25 minutes or until set. Allow to cool. Sift a little sugar over the top. Serve warm.
Serves 4

SPICED PRUNE CREAM

Metric/Imperial	American
225 g/8 oz large prunes, soaked overnight in water to cover	1¼ cups large prunes, soaked overnight in water to cover
1 × 5 cm/2 inch piece of cinnamon stick or 1 teaspoon ground cinnamon	1 × 2 inch piece of cinnamon stick, or 1 teaspoon ground cinnamon
175 ml/6 fl oz port	¾ cup port
25 g/1 oz icing sugar, sifted	¼ cup sifted confectioners' sugar
lemon juice (optional)	lemon juice (optional)
150 ml/¼ pint double cream	⅔ cup heavy cream
TO DECORATE:	TO DECORATE:
whipped cream	whipped cream
angelica leaves	angelica leaves

Place the prunes, water and cinnamon into a saucepan and cook gently until the prunes are tender. Strain and reduce the liquid to 4 tablespoons by rapid boiling. Stone (pit) the prunes. Fit the METAL BLADE.

Put the prunes into the processor bowl with the reduced liquid, port and sugar. Process until smooth.

Check sweetness and add more sugar if necessary.

If too sweet, add a little lemon juice. Turn the prune purée into a bowl. Whip the cream until thick and fold into the prunes. Pour into small pots and chill. Decorate with whipped cream piped into rosettes, and angelica.
Serves 6 to 8

PRUNE AND ALMOND FRITTERS

Metric/Imperial	American
25 large prunes, soaked overnight	25 large prunes, soaked overnight
120 ml/4 fl oz white wine	½ cup white wine
100 g/4 oz plain flour	1 cup all-purpose flour
pinch of salt	pinch of salt
grated rind of ½ lemon	grated rind of ½ lemon
25 blanched almonds	25 blanched almonds
1 egg white	1 egg white
oil or fat for deep-frying	oil or fat for deep-frying
2 tablespoons caster sugar	2 tablespoons sugar
1 teaspoon ground cinnamon	1 teaspoon ground cinnamon

Simmer the prunes in the soaking liquid until just tender. Drain. (Keep the liquid as slightly sweetened it makes a delicious drink.)

Fit the PLASTIC BLADE. Put the wine, flour, salt and lemon rind into the bowl and process until smooth. Turn into another bowl and rest the batter for 30 minutes.

Slit the prunes lengthwise, remove the stones (pits) and replace with an almond. Close over. Whisk the egg white until stiff but not dry and fold into the batter. Heat the oil or fat to 190°C/375°F. Dip each prune into the batter then place carefully into the oil or fat. Cook until golden. Drain on absorbent kitchen paper and turn onto a serving dish. Mix together the sugar and cinnamon and dust the prunes before serving.
Serves 4

BLACKBERRY AND PORT STREUSEL

Metric/Imperial	American
100 g/4 oz plain flour	1 cup all-purpose flour
75 g/3 oz chilled butter, cut into pieces	¼ cup plus 2 tablespoons chilled butter, cut into pieces
75 g/3 oz soft brown sugar	½ cup light brown sugar
450 g/1 lb blackberries, washed and picked over	4 cups blackberries, washed and picked over
4 tablespoons port	4 tablespoons port
50 g/2 oz caster sugar	¼ cup sugar
vanilla ice cream (page 87), to serve	vanilla ice cream (page 87), to serve

Fit the METAL BLADE. Put the flour into the processor bowl, add the butter and process until the mixture looks like fine crumbs. Add the brown sugar and blend, using 2 bursts of pulse action. Set aside.

Grease a 750 ml/1½ pint/3¾ cup ovenproof dish. Put in the blackberries, sprinkle with the port and lightly stir in the sugar. Sprinkle the 'streusel' evenly over the top. Bake in a moderately hot oven (190°C/375°F, Gas Mark 5) for about 30 minutes. Serve with vanilla ice cream.

Serves 4

ICED LEMON TORTE

Metric/Imperial	American
175 g/6 oz digestive biscuits, broken up	6 oz Graham crackers, broken up
3 eggs, separated	3 eggs, separated
grated rind and juice of 2 large lemons	grated rind and juice of 2 large lemons
150 g/5 oz caster sugar	⅔ cup sugar
pinch of salt	pinch of salt
250 ml/8 fl oz double cream	1 cup heavy cream

Fit the METAL BLADE. Put the biscuits (crackers) into the bowl and process to fine crumbs. Lightly butter a 20 cm/8 inch flan tin (pie pan) which is suitable for the freezer, and sprinkle two-thirds of the crumbs over the bottom and sides.

Place the yolks, lemon rind and juice, sugar and salt into the processor bowl and process until thick and light, scraping down the bowl once. Pour into another bowl.

Whip the cream until stiff and fold into the lemon mixture. Pour into the dish. Sprinkle the remaining crumbs over the top, then place in the freezer to freeze. Cover with foil to store in the freezer.

To serve, remove from the freezer 10 minutes before serving. The torte must not soften.

Serves 4

From left: Blackberry and Port Streusal and Blackberry Pudding

BLACKBERRY PUDDING

Metric/Imperial	American
225 g/8 oz blackberries washed and picked over	1 cup blackberries, washed and picked over
1 quantity Victoria sponge mixture (page 96)	1 quantity Victoria sponge mixture (page 96)
grated rind and juice of 1 lemon	grated rind and juice of 1 lemon

Grease a 900 ml/1½ pint/3¾ cup heatproof basin and put the blackberries in the bottom. Make up the Victoria sponge mixture adding the lemon rind and juice. Spoon the mixture over the blackberries and smooth the top. Cut a square of aluminium foil 15 cm/6 inch larger than the width of the basin and grease well. Cover the basin with the foil, pleating the foil across the top. Secure with string.

Place the basin in a pan of boiling water that comes half-way up the basin. Cover and cook over a gentle heat for about 2 hours or until the pudding is cooked. Top up with boiling water when necessary. Turn out and serve with pouring cream.

Serves 4 to 6

SOUFFLÉ LEMON PUDDING

Metric/Imperial	American
175 g/6 oz caster sugar	¾ cup sugar
4 eggs, separated	4 eggs, separated
2 teaspoons grated lemon rind	2 teaspoons grated lemon rind
3 tablespoons lemon juice	3 tablespoons lemon juice
pinch of salt	pinch of salt
3 tablespoons plain flour	3 tablespoons all-purpose flour
pinch of cream of tartar	pinch of cream of tartar
sifted icing sugar, to decorate	sifted confectioners' sugar, to decorate

Well grease a 1.75 litre/3 pint/7½ cup soufflé dish and dust it with a little of the sugar.

Fit the PLASTIC BLADE. Put the egg yolks, sugar, lemon rind and juice, salt and flour into the bowl and process until thick and light. Pour into a large bowl.

Put the egg whites into another large bowl, add the cream of tartar and beat until stiff but not dry. Take out one-quarter of the egg white and stir it well into the lemon mixture. Cut and fold in the remaining portion of egg white. Pour into the prepared dish. Stand the dish in a baking tin (pan) half filled with hot water. Bake in a moderate oven (160°C/325°F, Gas Mark 3) for about 40 to 45 minutes, or until well risen and golden. Allow to cool; the pudding will separate into two layers. Chill and serve dusted with icing (confectioners') sugar.

Serves 4 to 6

CHOCOLATE AND ALMOND MERINGUES

Metric/Imperial	American
50 g/2 oz blanched almonds	½ cup blanched almonds
50 g/2 oz plain chocolate, broken into pieces	2 squares semi-sweet chocolate, broken into pieces
4 egg whites	4 egg whites
pinch of cream of tartar	pinch of cream of tartar
225 g/8 oz caster sugar	1 cup sugar
few drops vanilla essence	few drops vanilla extract

Fit the GRATING DISC. Put the almonds into the feed tube and grate. Add the chocolate and grate. Mix the almonds and chocolate together in a small bowl and set aside.

Put the egg whites in a large bowl, add the cream of tartar and whisk until very stiff. Add half the sugar, whisk again until very thick and shiny. Cut and fold in the remaining sugar with the chocolate mixture and vanilla. Line a baking sheet with non-stick parchment. Shape the mixture into ovals, using two tablespoons, and drop gently on to the sheet. Bake in a cool oven (120°C/250°F, Gas Mark ½) for 1¼ hours. Turn off the heat and leave the meringues in the oven until cold. Serve dusted with icing sugar.

Makes 30 meringues

Note: The meringues can be sandwiched with sweetened whipped cream flavoured with melted chocolate or instant coffee powder.

QUICK CHOCOLATE CUSTARDS

Metric/Imperial	American
225 g/8 oz plain chocolate, broken into pieces	8 squares semi-sweet chocolate, broken into pieces
2 eggs	2 eggs
1 teaspoon vanilla essence	1 teaspoon vanilla extract
350 ml/12 fl oz milk	1½ cups milk
2 teaspoons instant coffee	2 teaspoons instant coffee
2 teaspoons gelatine	2 teaspoons unflavored gelatin

Fit the GRATING DISC. Put the chocolate in the feed tube and grate. Remove and set aside. Fit the Plastic blade.

Put the eggs and vanilla in the bowl and process. Bring the milk and chocolate almost to the boil. Dissolve the instant coffee and gelatine in the milk. Pour into processor bowl and combine with the eggs, using 3 or 4 bursts of pulse action.

Pour into 4 individual dishes and chill until set. Serve decorated with whipped cream.

Serves 4

APRICOT CRUNCH

Metric/Imperial	American
225 g/8 oz dried apricots, soaked	1¼ cups dried apricots, soaked
2 teaspoons gelatine	2 teaspoons unflavored gelatin
1 small can evaporated milk, chilled	1 small can evaporated milk, chilled
300 ml/½ pint natural yogurt	1¼ cups unflavored yogurt
50 g/2 oz blanched whole almonds	½ cup blanched whole almonds
3 tablespoons butter or margarine	3 tablespoons butter or margarine
50 g/2 oz demerara sugar	4 tablespoons brown sugar

Cook the apricots and their soaking liquid until tender. Drain and reserve the juice. Fit the METAL BLADE. Place the apricots in the bowl and purée.

Bring 4 tablespoons of the reserved juice to the boil and dissolve the gelatine in this. Pour through the feed tube and use pulse action to blend in.

Whisk the evaporated milk until thick and foamy.

Add the fruit purée, and fold in. Stir in the yogurt, pour into 6 individual dishes and chill.

Using pulse action, chop the nuts fairly finely. Melt the butter or margarine in a small pan and stir in the sugar. Cook slowly until the sugar dissolves and the mixture turns golden-brown. Stir in the nuts then pour onto a metal tray or sheet of foil with the edges turned up. Leave to cool. Break the toffee into small pieces and scatter over the top of the chilled desserts.
Serves 6

ORANGES WITH CARAMEL

Metric/Imperial	American
4 sweet oranges	4 sweet oranges
4 tablespoons orange juice	4 tablespoons orange juice
2 tablespoons Curaçao	2 tablespoons Curaçao
100 g/4 oz granulated sugar	$\frac{1}{2}$ cup sugar

Remove the rind from one of the oranges, making sure no pith remains. Cut into fine strips and blanch in boiling water for 1 minute. Cool under running water, drain and set aside.

Fit the SLICING DISC. Remove all the peel and pith from the oranges. Put into the feed tube and slice. Arrange the orange slices on an attractive heatproof dish.

Combine the orange juice and Curaçao and pour over the oranges. Cover and chill.

Gently heat the sugar in a small pan until it caramelizes to a golden colour. Make sure it does not burn. With a wooden spoon, shake drops of the caramel over the oranges. They will set into toffee.

Serve chilled with cream; garnish with the rind.
Serves 4

DUTCH BANANA CREAM

Metric/Imperial	American
225 g/8 oz bananas, weighed after peeling and cut into pieces	$\frac{1}{2}$ lb bananas, weighed after peeling, and cut into pieces
50 g/2 oz caster sugar	$\frac{1}{4}$ cup sugar
100 g/4 oz cream cheese	$\frac{1}{2}$ cup cream cheese
grated rind and juice of 1 lemon	grated rind and juice of 1 lemon
1 tablespoon gelatine	1 tablespoon unflavored gelatin
2 tablespoons water	
1 tablespoon kirsch	2 tablespoons water
toasted flaked almonds, to decorate	1 tablespoon kirsch
sponge fingers, to serve	toasted flaked almonds, to decorate
	ladyfingers, to serve

Fit the PLASTIC BLADE. Put the bananas, sugar, cream cheese, rind and lemon juice into the processor bowl. Sprinkle the gelatine over the water in a small bowl and leave to swell. Place over a pan of hot water and stir until dissolved. Pour into banana mixture together with the kirsch. Process until smooth, about 10 to 15 seconds. Pour into 4 glass goblets and chill. Decorate with the almonds and serve with sponge fingers (ladyfingers).
Serves 4

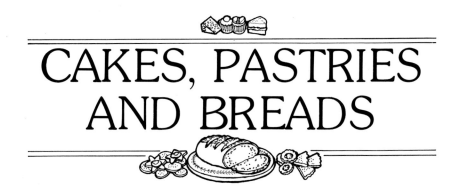

CAKES, PASTRIES AND BREADS

The aroma of baking is guaranteed to draw family and friends
straight to the kitchen to wait for the treat from the oven.
If you have never been a successful baker or pastry maker, a food
processor is marvellous and makes cakes, pastries, breads and
biscuits (cookies) in a moment.

Most cakes are made using the plastic blade and it is
important to follow the processing time exactly. Overprocessing
tends to beat the air out of the mixture and can result in
a heavy, close-textured cake. If you are creaming butter and sugar
it is important to have the butter at room temperature so
that a fluffy light cream results, not crumbly bits of butter rolled
in sugar.

Pastries are made using the metal blade and are ready as soon as
the mixture forms a ball around the blade. Shortcrust pastry
(basic pie dough) is made in seconds. Choux pastry (paste) takes a
few minutes, as it involves heating the milk and melting
the butter.

Breads are wonderful to make in a processor and there are
two simple stages. The yeast mixture and liquid are processed into
the dough, the dough is set aside to rise, then returned to
the bowl to be kneaded. The dough is then treated in the usual way.

Biscuits (cookies) and scones (biscuits) are all speedily prepared in the food processor. Shortbread cookies are particularly
successful as are refrigerator biscuits (cookies).

Scones (Biscuits) (page 109),
Croissants (page 103) and
Spicy Flapjacks (page 104)

SODA CAKE

Metric/Imperial	American
175 g/6 oz plain flour	1½ cups all-purpose flour
¼ teaspoon mixed spice	¼ teaspoon mixed spice
½ teaspoon bicarbonate of soda	½ teaspoon baking soda
½ teaspoon baking powder	½ teaspoon baking powder
50 g/2 oz butter	¼ cup butter
50 g/2 oz lard	¼ cup shortening
50 g/2 oz stoned dates	⅓ cup pitted dates
50 g/2 oz walnut pieces	½ cup walnut pieces
75 g/3 oz caster sugar	¼ cup plus 2 tablespoons sugar
120 ml/4 fl oz milk	½ cup milk
50 g/2 oz seedless raisins	⅓ cup pitted raisins

Fit the METAL BLADE. Sieve the flour, spice, soda and baking powder together. Put into the bowl and add the butter, lard (shortening), dates, walnuts and sugar.

Process until the mixture resembles fine crumbs. Pour in the milk, add the raisins and blend with 4 bursts of pulse action. Grease an 18 × 10 cm/7 × 4 inch loaf tin (pan), and pour in the mixture. Bake in a moderate oven (180°C/350°F, Gas Mark 4) for 1 hour or until firm to the touch. Leave to cool for a few minutes in the tin (pan). Cool on a cake rack.

Makes one 18 × 10 cm/7 × 4 inch cake

VICTORIA SPONGE

Metric/Imperial	American
SPONGE:	SPONGE:
100 g/4 oz soft margarine	½ cup soft margarine
100 g/4 oz caster sugar	½ cup sugar
100 g/4 oz self-raising flour	1 cup self-rising flour
1 teaspoon baking powder	1 teaspoon baking powder
2 eggs	2 eggs
1 tablespoon warm water	1 tablespoon warm water
FILLING:	FILLING:
2 tablespoons strawberry jam	2 tablespoons strawberry jelly
60 ml/2 fl oz double cream, whipped	¼ cup heavy cream, whipped
TO DECORATE:	TO DECORATE:
1 tablespoon icing sugar	1 tablespoon sifted confectioners' sugar

Grease and base line an 18 cm/7 inch deep cake tin (pan) and set the oven temperature to moderate (180°C/350°F, Gas Mark 4).

Fit the PLASTIC BLADE. Place all the ingredients for the sponge in the bowl and process for 10 seconds. Clean down the bowl and process for a further 10 seconds.

Pour the batter into the prepared tin (pan) and bake in a preheated moderate oven for 30 minutes or until firm to a light touch. Turn onto a wire rack and leave to cool.

When the cake is completely cold, split and fill with the jam (jelly) and cream. Replace the top and dredge with sugar.

Makes one 18 cm/7 inch round cake

COUNTRY CAKE

Metric/Imperial	American
225 g/8 oz self-raising flour	2 cups self-rising flour
100 g/4 oz butter	½ cup butter
150 g/5 oz granulated sugar	⅔ cup sugar
½ teaspoon mixed spice	½ teaspoon mixed spice
2 eggs	2 eggs
5 tablespoons milk	⅓ cup milk
1 tablespoon vinegar	1 tablespoon vinegar
150 g/5 oz mixed dried fruit	1 cup mixed dried fruit

Fit the PLASTIC BLADE. Put the flour, butter, sugar and spice into the processor bowl. Process until the mixture resembles fine breadcrumbs. Add the eggs, milk, vinegar and fruit. Blend with 4 bursts of pulse action. Pour into a greased 18 cm/7 inch round cake tin (pan). Bake in a moderate oven (180°C/350°F, Gas Mark 4) for 1 hour or until firm to the touch. Turn onto a cake rack to cool.

Makes one 18 cm/7 inch round cake

Variations

CHERRY AND ALMOND CAKE

Metric/Imperial	American
50 g/2 oz ground almonds	½ cup ground almonds
100 g/4 oz glacé cherries	½ cup candied cherries
½ teaspoon almond essence	½ teaspoon almond extract
few flaked almonds, to decorate	few flaked almonds, to decorate

Proceed as for Country Cake substituting the above ingredients for the dried fruit and spice. Decorate with a few flaked almonds sprinkled over the mixture before baking.

GINGER AND LEMON CAKE

Metric/Imperial	American
75 g/3 oz crystallized ginger	½ cup candied ginger
1 teaspoon ground ginger	1 teaspoon ground ginger
grated rind and juice of 1 lemon	grated rind and juice of 1 lemon

Proceed as for Country Cake substituting the above ingredients for the dried fruit and spice. Add the lemon juice with the liquid ingredients.

DANISH CHEESECAKE

Metric/Imperial	American
175 g/6 oz carrots, washed and lightly scraped	6 oz carrots, washed and lightly scraped
150 g/5 oz unsalted butter	⅔ cup sweet butter
200 g/7 oz caster sugar	⅞ cup sugar
pinch of salt	pinch of salt
2 eggs	2 eggs
200 g/7 oz plain flour	1¾ cups all-purpose flour
1 teaspoon ground cinnamon	1 teaspoon ground cinnamon
1 teaspoon baking powder	1 teaspoon baking powder
100 g/4 oz seedless raisins	⅔ cup seedless raisins
ICING:	FROSTING:
50 g/2 oz unsalted butter, at room temperature	¼ cup sweet butter, at room temperature
90 g/3½ oz cream cheese	½ cup cream cheese
100 g/4 oz icing sugar, sifted	1 cup sifted confectioners' sugar
½ teaspoon vanilla essence	½ teaspoon vanilla extract

Fit the GRATING DISC and use to grate the carrots. Set aside. Melt the butter gently.

Fit the PLASTIC BLADE. Put the sugar, salt, melted butter, grated carrots and eggs into the processor bowl and process for about 20 seconds. Sift the flour with the cinnamon and baking powder and add to the bowl with the raisins. Use 4 bursts of pulse action to combine. Pour into a greased 16 × 20 cm/6½ × 8 inch loaf tin (pan). Bake in a moderate oven (160°C/325°F, Gas Mark 3) for 45 minutes or until firm to a light touch. Allow the cake to cool a little in the tin (pan) before turning onto a cake rack.

Prepare the icing (frosting). Put the butter and cream cheese into the processor bowl and process for 10 seconds. Add the sugar and vanilla and process until well mixed. Leave the cake bottom side up. Spread the icing (frosting) over the top and sides and make a decorative pattern with a fork.

Makes one 16 × 20 cm/6½ × 8 inch cake

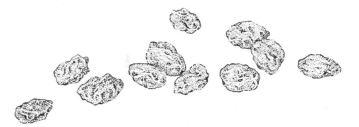

VIENNA CAKES

Metric/Imperial	American
175 g/6 oz soft margarine	¾ cup soft margarine
200 g/7 oz plain flour	1¾ cups all-purpose flour
few drops vanilla essence	few drops vanilla extract
75 g/3 oz icing sugar, sifted	⅔ cup sifted confectioners' sugar
raspberry jam	raspberry jelly

Fit the PLASTIC BLADE. Put the margarine, flour, vanilla and 50 g/2 oz/½ cup of the sugar into the bowl. Process for 30 seconds until light and fluffy. Transfer the mixture to a piping (pastry) bag fitted with a fluted 1 cm/½ inch nozzle. Line a patty (tartlet) pan with paper cake cases. Pipe the mixture into each case and leave a slight dent in the centre. Bake in a moderate oven (190°C/375°F, Gas Mark 5) for 10 to 12 minutes. Leave to cool. Sift the remaining sugar over the top and drop a spot of jam (jelly) into the centres.

Makes 10 to 12

CHOCOLATE BRANDY CAKE

Metric/Imperial	American
100 g/4 oz butter	½ cup butter
100 g/4 oz caster sugar	½ cup sugar
grated rind of ½ an orange and ½ a lemon	grated rind of ½ an orange and ½ a lemon
2 eggs	2 eggs
50 g/2 oz sweetened drinking chocolate	½ cup sweetened cocoa powder
100 g/4 oz ground almonds	1 cup ground almonds
50 g/2 oz self-raising flour	½ cup self-rising flour
1 tablespoon brandy	1 tablespoon brandy

Fit the PLASTIC BLADE. Put the butter and sugar in the bowl and process until light and fluffy. Add the orange and lemon rinds and eggs and process until well mixed, about 10 seconds. Add the chocolate (cocoa) and almonds and process until well mixed. Add the flour and brandy and mix with 3 or 4 bursts of pulse action. Scrape down the bowl and give 2 further bursts. Pour into a greased and bottom lined 15 cm/6 inch round cake tin (pan). Bake in a moderate oven (180°C/350°F, Gas Mark 4) for 1 hour or until the cake is firm to the touch.

Makes one 15 cm/6 inch round cake

CHOCOLATE TOFFEE CAKE

Metric/Imperial	American
75 g/3 oz plain chocolate, broken into pieces	3 squares semi-sweet chocolate, broken into pieces
100 g/4 oz butter	½ cup butter
100 g/4 oz soft brown sugar	⅔ cup brown sugar
2 eggs	2 eggs
50 g/2 oz self-raising flour	½ cup self-rising flour
50 g/2 oz ground almonds	½ cup ground almonds
TOFFEE ICING:	TOFFEE FROSTING:
50 g/2 oz butter	¼ cup butter
100 g/4 oz soft brown sugar	⅔ cup brown sugar
2 tablespoons golden syrup	2 tablespoons maple syrup
120 ml/4 fl oz double cream	½ cup heavy cream
icing sugar (optional)	confectioners' sugar (optional)

Fit the GRATING DISC. Drop chocolate into feed tube and grate, set aside. Fit the PLASTIC BLADE. Put the butter and sugar into bowl and process until light and fluffy. Add eggs and process again until well incorporated. Add the flour and ground almonds to the bowl and incorporate, using 2 bursts of pulse action. Add the chocolate and give 2 more bursts of pulse action. Pour into a greased 15 cm/6 inch round cake tin (pan). Bake in a moderate oven (180°C/350°F, Gas Mark 4) for 1¼ hours or until firm to a light touch. Leave in tin (pan) for 5 minutes and then turn carefully onto a wire rack to cool.

Prepare the toffee icing. Put the sugar, butter and syrup in a small pan. Stir well together over a gentle heat until the sugar is dissolved. Bring to the boil, reduce heat immediately and simmer, without stirring, for 5 minutes. Remove from the heat and slowly add the cream in a steady stream, beating well with a wooden spoon. Leave the icing (frosting) to cool and thicken. Spread over the top and sides of the cake. If you prefer a thicker icing (frosting) on your cake beat in sufficient icing (confectioners') sugar until the mixture forms soft peaks. Spread over the cake and pull into rough peaks. The top can be finished with a little extra grated chocolate if liked.

Makes one 15 cm/6 inch round cake

Right: Vienna Cakes and Chocolate Toffee Cake

CHOUX PASTRY (PASTE)

Metric/Imperial	American
200 ml/⅓ pint water	⅞ cup water
75 g/3 oz butter	¼ cup plus 2 tablespoons butter
100 g/4 oz plain flour	1 cup all-purpose flour
pinch of salt	pinch of salt
3 eggs	3 eggs

Fit the PLASTIC BLADE. Heat the water and butter in a small pan over a gentle heat. Place the flour and salt in the bowl. When the butter has melted, bring to the boil. Switch the machine on and pour the boiling liquid through the feed tube. Process for 12 seconds. Add the eggs, one at a time, and process for 3 seconds after each addition. The paste should be shining. If not, process a few seconds longer.

Fit a piping (pastry) bag with a plain 1 cm/½ inch nozzle and pipe small rounds or fingers on a greased baking sheet. Bake in a moderately hot oven (200°C/400°F, Gas Mark 6) for 30 to 40 minutes or until golden, light and hollow sounding when tapped. They must be well cooked or the buns or fingers will collapse when removed from the oven. Cool on a cake rack. These puffs can be used for sweet or savoury dishes.
Makes 20 to 30 fingers or rounds

CHOCOLATE PROFITEROLES
Fill the split puffs with sweetened whipped cream. Dust with a little sifted icing (confectioners') sugar and serve with hot chocolate sauce.

ROUGH PUFF PASTRY (PASTE)

Metric/Imperial	American
225 g/8 oz plain flour	2 cups all-purpose flour
½ teaspoon cream of tartar	½ teaspoon cream of tartar
pinch of salt	pinch of salt
200 g/7 oz chilled butter, cut into 2.5 cm/1 inch cubes	⅞ cup chilled butter, cut into 1 inch cubes
150 ml/¼ pint iced water	⅔ cup iced water

Fit the PLASTIC BLADE. Place all the ingredients into the processor bowl and process for about 10 seconds or until the mixture forms a ball. Turn the dough (paste) onto a surface well dusted with flour. Flour the rolling pin and lightly roll pastry (paste) out until it is 1 cm/½ inch thick. Fold the bottom third of the pastry (dough) up then the top third down. Seal the edges lightly and chill for 20 minutes. Repeat the rolling, folding and chilling 2 more times. Roll out and use as directed.
Makes about 450 g/1 lb

SHORTCRUST PASTRY (BASIC PIE DOUGH)

Metric/Imperial	American
225 g/8 oz plain flour	2 cups all-purpose flour
pinch of salt	pinch of salt
150 g/5 oz butter	½ cup plus 2 tablespoons butter
1 egg	1 egg
1 tablespoon cold water	1 tablespoon cold water

Fit the METAL BLADE. Put the flour, salt and butter into the bowl. Process until the mixture resembles fine breadcrumbs. Add the egg and water and blend until the mixture forms a ball, using 4 bursts of pulse action. Wrap in cling film (plastic wrap) and chill. Roll out and use as directed.
Makes 225 g/8 oz/½ lb

SWEET SHORTCRUST PASTRY (SWEET BASIC PIE DOUGH)

Metric/Imperial	American
225 g/8 oz plain flour	2 cups all-purpose flour
pinch of salt	pinch of salt
150 g/5 oz butter	½ cup plus 2 tablespoons butter
1 egg	1 egg
1 tablespoon cold water	1 tablespoon cold water
40 g/1½ oz caster sugar	3 tablespoons sugar

Fit the METAL BLADE. Put the flour, salt and butter into the bowl. Process until the mixture resembles fine breadcrumbs. Beat the egg and water together and stir in the sugar. Pour into the processor bowl and blend until the mixture forms a ball, using 4 bursts of pulse action. Wrap in cling film (plastic wrap) and chill. Roll out and use as directed.
Makes 225 g/8 oz/½ lb

CHEESE PASTRY (PASTE)

Metric/Imperial	American
100 g/4 oz mature Cheddar cheese	¼ lb mature Cheddar cheese
225 g/8 oz plain flour	2 cups all-purpose flour
pinch of salt	pinch of salt
pinch of cayenne pepper	pinch of cayenne pepper
150 g/5 oz butter	½ cup plus 2 tablespoons butter
1 egg	1 egg
1 tablespoon cold water	1 tablespoon cold water

Fit the GRATING DISC and use to grate the cheese. Set aside. Fit the METAL BLADE. Put the flour, salt, cayenne pepper and butter into the processor bowl. Process until the mixture resembles fine breadcrumbs. Add the egg, cheese and water and blend until the mixture forms a ball, using 4 bursts of pulse action. Wrap in cling film (plastic wrap) and chill.

If the cheese is really well flavoured, this pastry makes very good cheese straws. For variety, add 1 tablespoon of walnuts with the flour.
Makes about 450 g/1 lb

GÂTEAU BASQUE

Metric/Imperial	American
225 g/8 oz sweet shortcrust pastry (page 101)	½ lb sweet basic pie dough (page 101)
1 tablespoon dark rum	1 tablespoon dark rum
few drops almond essence	few drops almond extract
Créme Pâtissière, omit the vanilla essence (page 54)	Créme Pâtissière, omit the vanilla extract (page 54)
1 × 400 g/14 oz can pears, drained or 450 g/1 lb fresh pears, peeled and poached	1 × 14 oz can pears, drained or 1 lb fresh pears, peeled and poached
caster sugar	sugar

Divide the pastry (dough) in half. Roll out one half and use to line an 18 cm/7 inch flan tin (pie pan). Stir the rum and almond essence (extract) into the Créme Pâtissière and pour into the case (shell). Arrange the pears, cut side down, on the filling with the pointed ends to the centre. Roll out the second piece of pastry (dough). Dampen the rim of the case (shell) and cover with the pastry (dough). Crimp the edges. Brush the top with a little water and sprinkle with caster sugar. Make a few slits on top. Bake in a moderately hot oven (200°C/400°F, Gas Mark 6) for 10 minutes. Then reduce the heat to 180°C/350°F, Gas Mark 4 until golden brown. Serve warm or chilled.
Serves 6

BANBURYS

Metric/Imperial	American
150 g/5 oz currants	1 cup currants
1 teaspoon mixed spice	1 teaspoon apple pie spice
75 g/3 oz soft brown sugar	½ cup light brown sugar
50 g/2 oz butter	¼ cup butter
1 teaspoon flour	1 teaspoon flour
1 tablespoon rum (optional)	1 tablespoon rum (optional)
450 g/1 lb rough puff pastry (page 100)	1 lb rough puff paste (page 100)
caster sugar, for sprinkling	sugar, for sprinkling

Fit the PLASTIC BLADE. Process the currants, spice, sugar, butter, flour and rum for 20 seconds.

Roll out the pastry (paste) on a floured board until it is about 3 mm/⅛ inch thick. Cut out saucer-sized circles. Gather the trimmings, roll out and cut.

Divide the filling equally between the circles, placing it in the centres. Dampen the rims with water and gather up the pastry into the centre and pinch well together. Turn the pastries over and roll each one into an oval. Slash the top of each banbury. Place on a dampened baking sheet. Bake in a hot oven (220°C/425°F, Gas Mark 7) for 15 minutes. Remove, brush with a little water and sprinkle with sugar. Return to the oven to crystallize for about 5 minutes. Cool on a wire cake rack.
Makes 6 to 8 banburys

CROISSANTS

Metric/Imperial	American
2 teaspoons dried yeast	2 teaspoons dried yeast
1 teaspoon sugar	1 teaspoon sugar
250 ml/8 fl oz hand-hot water	1 cup hand-hot water
550 g/1¼ lb plain flour	5 cups all-purpose flour
225 g/8 oz chilled butter or margarine, cut into 1.5 cm/½ inch cubes	1 cup butter or margarine, cut into ½ inch cubes
175 ml/6 fl oz evaporated milk	¾ cup evaporated milk
50 g/2 oz sugar	¼ cup sugar
1½ teaspoons salt	1½ teaspoons salt
1 egg	1 egg
50 g/2 oz butter or margarine, melted and cooled	¼ cup butter or margarine, melted and cooled
TO GLAZE:	TO GLAZE:
1 small egg, mixed with a little water	1 small egg, mixed with a little water

Dissolve the yeast and sugar in the water and leave in a warm place for 10 minutes or until frothy.

Fit the METAL BLADE. Put 450 g/1 lb/4 cups of the flour in the processor bowl and sprinkle the butter or margarine cubes over it. Using pulse action, mix with several bursts until the butter or margarine pieces are the size of haricot (navy) beans. Tip into a large bowl.

Pour the yeast mixture into the processor bowl. Add the milk, salt, sugar, egg, remaining flour, and the melted and cooled butter or margarine. Process until the mixture is smooth.

Pour the yeast batter over the flour mixture in the bowl and with a metal palette knife, turn over carefully until all the flour is moistened, but no longer. Cover bowl with plastic cling film (wrap) and put into the refrigerator, or cool larder, for at least 4 hours (or as long as 4 days).

Turn out on to a lightly floured board and shape into a ball. Knead briefly. Cut into 4 pieces and put 3 back in the refrigerator. Roll out the remaining piece into an oblong about 45 × 23 cm/18 × 9 inches. From this oblong cut out 8 equal triangles. Starting with the wide end of one triangle, roll up loosely, stretching slightly as you roll. On the last roll, curve into a crescent and place on an ungreased baking sheet. Make all the croissants in the same way, placing them 4 cm/1¼ inches apart on the sheet. Cover lightly (an inverted baking tin (pan) is excellent for this) and leave to rise at room temperature until doubled.

Brush with the egg and water mixture and bake in a moderate oven (160°C/325°F, Gas Mark 3) for 25 to 30 minutes. Place on rack to cool and reheat quickly in a hot oven when ready to serve; or cool and freeze.

Makes 32 croissants

From left: Gâteau Basque and Banburys

103

SPICY FLAPJACKS

Metric/Imperial	American
225 g/8 oz porridge oats	2¼ cups porridge oats
100 g/4 oz dark brown Barbados or Muscovado sugar	⅔ cup light brown sugar
1 teaspoon ground ginger	1 teaspoon ground ginger
75 g/3 oz butter or margarine, melted	¼ cup plus 2 tablespoons butter or margarine, melted
¼ teaspoon salt	¼ teaspoon salt

Fit the METAL BLADE. Put all the ingredients in the processor bowl and process for about 30 seconds. Press the mixture in a layer, about 1 cm/½ inch thick, into a well-greased 18 cm/7 inch square cake tin (pan). Bake in a moderate oven (180°C/350°F, Gas Mark 4) for about 45 minutes or until brown and firm. Mark into squares in the tin (pan) while still warm. Leave to cool before removing.

Makes approximately 20 squares

CARAWAY AND HERB SODA BREAD

Metric/Imperial	American
25 g/1 oz mixed fresh herbs, leaves only (marjoram, parsley, chives, basil and rosemary or 1 teaspoon of dried herbs)	1 oz mixed fresh herbs, leaves only (marjoram, parsley, chives, basil and rosemary or 1 teaspoon of dried herbs)
100 g/4 oz wholemeal flour	1 cup wholewheat flour
100 g/4 oz plain flour	1 cup all-purpose flour
½ teaspoon bicarbonate of soda	½ teaspoon baking soda
½ teaspoon salt	½ teaspoon salt
50 g/2 oz butter, cut into 4 pieces	¼ cup butter, cut into 4 pieces
1 teaspoon cream of tartar	1 teaspoon cream of tartar
150 ml/¼ pint milk	⅔ cup milk
1 egg, beaten	1 egg, beaten
1 teaspoon caraway seeds	1 teaspoon caraway seeds

Fit the METAL BLADE. Place the herbs and wholemeal (wholewheat) flour into the bowl. Sift together the plain flour, bicarbonate of soda and salt, and add to the bowl. Process for 10 seconds to chop the herbs.

Add the butter and process to fine crumbs. Stir the cream of tartar into the milk. Add to the bowl and process until the mixture just forms a ball. Knead lightly on a floured surface into a round shape. Brush the top with the egg, and sprinkle over the caraway seeds. Cut into four pieces. Cook on a floured baking sheet in a moderately hot oven (200°C/400°F, Gas Mark 6) for about 25 minutes. Tap the bottom – if it sounds hollow it is cooked. Cool on a wire tray.

Makes 4 pieces

WHITE BREAD

Metric/Imperial	American
750 g/1½ lb strong white flour	6 cups white bread flour
15 g/½ oz lard	1 tablespoon shortening
2 teaspoons dried yeast	2 teaspoons dried yeast
400 ml/14 fl oz hand-hot water	1¾ cups hand-hot water
½ teaspoon caster sugar	½ teaspoon sugar

Fit the METAL BLADE. Put the flour and lard (shortening) in the processor bowl and blend for 30 seconds. Mix the yeast well with the warm water and sugar. Pour through the feed tube and process until the mixture forms a ball around the blade. Scrape out with the plastic spatula into a warmed, greased bowl. Turn the dough so it is greased on all surfaces. Cover and put in a warm place to rise until double in bulk, about 1 to 1¼ hours.

Return the dough to the processor bowl and process for 20 seconds to knead. Turn out onto a floured surface and shape into 1 large loaf or 2 small ones. Put into well greased 1 × 1 kg/2 lb or 2 × 450 g/1 lb bread tins (pans). Cover and leave until the dough has risen to the top of the tin (pan). Do not let the dough over-rise. Bake in a hot oven (230°C/450°F, Gas Mark 8) for 35 minutes or until well risen and golden. The dough should sound hollow when tapped. Cool on a wire rack.

Makes 1 × 1 kg/2 lb loaf or 2 × 450 g/1 lb loaves

DARK STICKY GINGERBREAD

Metric/Imperial	American
225 g/8 oz plain flour	2 cups all-purpose flour
1 teaspoon bicarbonate of soda	1 teaspoon baking soda
2 teaspoons ground ginger	2 teaspoons ground ginger
100 g/4 oz butter	½ cup butter
100 g/4 oz dark Barbados sugar	⅔ cup dark brown sugar
2 eggs, beaten	2 eggs, beaten
275 g/10 oz black treacle	⅞ cup molasses
50 g/2 oz sultanas or seedless raisins	⅓ cup seedless white raisins or raisins
50 g/2 oz chopped preserved ginger in syrup or chopped crystalized ginger	⅓ cup chopped preserved ginger in syrup or chopped candied ginger
2 tablespoons milk	2 tablespoons milk

Sift together the flour, soda and ground ginger. Fit the PLASTIC BLADE.

Place the butter and sugar in the bowl and process for 1 minute. Scrape down the bowl and process again for 20 seconds. Add the eggs and process for 20 seconds. Tip in the flour mixture and process for 10 seconds. Scrape the bowl down, add the treacle (molasses) and process for 10 seconds. Scrape bowl again and process for a further 10 seconds. Add the sultanas (seedless white raisins) or raisins, ginger and milk and give 3 bursts of pulse action. Pour the mixture into a greased and floured 15 cm/6 inch square cake tin (pan). Bake in a moderate oven (160°C/325°F, Gas Mark 3) for 1 hour. Reduce the heat to 180°C/300°F, Gas Mark 2 and cover the top of cake with greaseproof or brown paper. Bake for a further 30 minutes. Leave in the tin for at least 5 minutes before turning it onto a wire rack to cool.

When completely cold, wrap closely in cling film (plastic wrap) and foil. Store for at least 3 days before cutting. The cake is better if left for a week, the longer the better.

Makes one 15 cm/6 inch square cake

RICH MALT LOAF

Metric/Imperial	American
25 g/1 oz fresh yeast or 3 teaspoons dried	1 cake compressed yeast or 3 teaspoons dried
pinch of sugar	pinch of sugar
450 ml/¾ pint warm water	2 cups warm water
450 g/1 lb strong white flour	4 cups bread or all-purpose flour
1 teaspoon salt	1 teaspoon salt
2 tablespoons black treacle	2 tablespoons molasses
3 tablespoons malt extract	3 tablespoons malt extract
25 g/1 oz butter	2 tablespoons butter
175 g/6 oz sultanas	1 cup seedless white raisins
50 g/2 oz mixed chopped peel	⅓ cup mixed chopped peel

Cream fresh (compressed) yeast with the sugar. Stir in 150 ml/¼ pint/⅔ cup of the warm water. If using dried yeast, dissolve the yeast and sugar in 150 ml/¼ pint/⅔ cup of the warm water and leave for 10 minutes or until frothy.

In a small pan, gently heat together the treacle (molasses), malt and butter, stirring to combine. Allow to cool.

Fit the METAL BLADE. Place the flour and salt in the bowl and process for 2 seconds. With the machine running, pour the yeast liquid, remaining water and butter mixture through the feed tube. Process for about 20 seconds. Add the fruit and peel and incorporate, using 3 or 4 bursts of pulse action.

Divide the dough in half. Roll each half into an oblong and fold in three. Place each loaf into a greased 20 × 10 cm/8 × 4 inch loaf tin (pan). Cover and leave to rise in a warm place. The dough should almost reach the top of the tin (pan). Bake in a moderately hot oven (200°C/400°F, Gas Mark 6) for about 45 minutes. Cool on a rack. Serve in thick slices, generously buttered.

Makes two 20 × 10 cm/8 × 4 inch loaves

PITCAITHLY BANNOCKS

Metric/Imperial	American
1 batch unbaked shortbread mixture (below)	1 batch unbaked shortbread mixture (below)
2 teaspoons grated orange rind	2 teaspoons grated orange rind
25 g/1 oz flaked almonds	¼ cup flaked almonds

Prepare the shortbread mixture in the food processor, adding most of the orange rind with the sugar, and chill. Roll out to 5 mm/¼ inch thickness. Cut into rounds using a floured 6 cm/2½ inch round cutter. Place on a greased baking sheet.

Combine the remaining rind and almonds and sprinkle each bannock with a little of the mixture. Bake in a moderately hot oven (190 C/375 F, Gas Mark 5) for 20 minutes or until the edges are lightly coloured. Cool on the baking sheet.

Makes approximately 20 to 30 bannocks

Fit the METAL BLADE. Put the butter and sugar into the processor bowl and process until light and fluffy. Add the flour and blend until the mixture just forms a ball using 5 or 6 bursts of pulse action. Wrap the paste in cling film (plastic wrap) and chill.

Roll out the paste to 5 mm/¼ inch thickness. Cut out rounds, using a floured 6 cm/2½ inch round cutter. Place on a lightly greased baking sheet and bake in a moderately hot oven (190 C/375 F, Gas Mark 5) for about 20 minutes or until the edges are lightly coloured. Slide a thin palette knife under the biscuits (cookies) to loosen. Leave on the tray to cool and become crisp. Dust with a little sugar and store in an airtight tin.

Makes 20 to 30 biscuits (cookies)

From left: Pitcaithly Bannocks, Shortbread Cookies, Lemon Fingers and Peanut Butter Slices

SHORTBREAD COOKIES

Metric/Imperial	American
175 g/6 oz butter, at room temperature	¾ cup butter, at room temperature
75 g/3 oz caster sugar	6 tablespoons sugar
225 g/8 oz plain flour, sifted	2 cups all-purpose flour, sifted
a little extra caster sugar, for dusting	a little extra sugar, for dusting

PEANUT BUTTER SLICES

Metric/Imperial	American
1 batch unbaked shortbread mixture (below left)	1 batch unbaked shortbread mixture (below left)
225 g/8 oz crunchy peanut butter	1 cup ($\frac{1}{2}$ lb) crunchy peanut butter
225 g/8 oz seedless raisins	1$\frac{1}{3}$ cups seedless raisins
225 g/8 oz icing sugar, sifted	1$\frac{3}{4}$ cups sifted confectioners' sugar
75–150 g/3–5 oz butter, melted	$\frac{1}{3}$–$\frac{2}{3}$ cup butter, melted
175 g/6 oz plain chocolate cake covering	6 squares semi-sweet chocolate

Fit the PLASTIC BLADE. Pat the shortbread mixture into a 29 × 19 cm/11$\frac{1}{2}$ × 7$\frac{1}{2}$ inch shallow baking tin (pan). Bake in a moderately hot oven (190 C/375 F, Gas Mark 5) for about 20 minutes.

Put the peanut butter, raisins and sugar into the processor bowl and process for 10 seconds. Add 75 g/3 oz of the butter to the bowl and process until the mixture forms a soft ball, about 10 seconds. Add more of the melted butter if necessary. Spread the raisin mixture over the cooked shortbread and leave to set. Melt the chocolate slowly in a bowl over a pan of hot water. Spread over the cake and leave until set. Cut into 16 slices.

LEMON FINGERS

Metric/Imperial	American
BASE:	BASE:
175 g/6 oz plain flour	1$\frac{1}{2}$ cups all-purpose flour
100 g/4 oz butter	$\frac{1}{2}$ cup butter
50 g/2 oz icing sugar, sifted	$\frac{1}{2}$ cup sifted confectioners' sugar

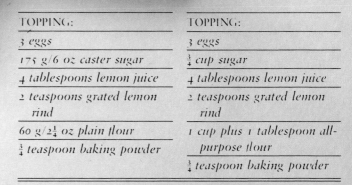

Metric/Imperial	American
TOPPING:	TOPPING:
3 eggs	3 eggs
175 g/6 oz caster sugar	$\frac{3}{4}$ cup sugar
4 tablespoons lemon juice	4 tablespoons lemon juice
2 teaspoons grated lemon rind	2 teaspoons grated lemon rind
60 g/2$\frac{1}{4}$ oz plain flour	1 cup plus 1 tablespoon all-purpose flour
$\frac{3}{4}$ teaspoon baking powder	$\frac{3}{4}$ teaspoon baking powder

Fit the METAL BLADE. Put all the ingredients for the Base into the bowl. Process until it forms a ball around the blade. Pat the pastry into a greased 20 cm/8 inch square shallow cake tin (pan). Bake in a moderately hot oven (190 C/375 F, Gas Mark 5) for 10 to 15 minutes or until light golden brown. Remove from the oven and allow to cool slightly.

Put all the ingredients for the Topping into the bowl and process for 6 seconds. Pour the mixture over the base and bake for a further 20 minutes or until golden brown; do not over bake. Allow to cool in the tin (pan) and cut into fingers. Icing (confectioners') sugar can be sifted over the top.
Makes 32 fingers

CHEESE THINS

Metric/Imperial	American
225 g/8 oz mature Cheddar cheese, chilled	½ lb mature Cheddar cheese, chilled
350 g/12 oz plain flour	3 cups all-purpose flour
1 teaspoon salt	1 teaspoon salt
225 g/8 oz butter or margarine	1 cup butter or margarine
good pinch cayenne pepper	good pinch cayenne pepper
½ teaspoon dried dill weed, or 1 teaspoon caraway seeds, or 1 teaspoon celery seeds	½ teaspoon dried dill weed, or 1 teaspoon caraway seeds, or 1 teaspoon celery seeds
1–2 tablespoons milk (optional)	1–2 tablespoons milk (optional)

Fit the GRATING DISC and use to grate the cheese. Set aside.

Fit the METAL BLADE. Put the flour, salt and butter or margarine into the bowl. Process to fine breadcrumbs. Add the cheese, cayenne and choice of herb and mix, using 2 or 3 bursts of pulse action. Add the milk if necessary.

Form the mixture into a ball on a sheet of greaseproof (wax) paper. Cut in two and form each half into a roll about 5 cm/2 inch in diameter. Wrap in cling film (plastic wrap) and chill well for about 3 hours. With a sharp knife cut the mixture into very thin slices about 3 mm/⅛ inch thick.

Place on a lightly oiled baking sheet and bake in a moderate oven (180°C/350°F, Gas Mark 4) for about 10 to 12 minutes until light brown. Take care not to overbake as these will burn easily. Cool on a cake rack and store in an air tight container.
Makes approximately 40 cheese thins

LEMON CRISPIES

Metric/Imperial	American
175 g/6 oz butter, at room temperature	¾ cup butter, at room temperature
50 g/2 oz icing sugar, sifted	½ cup sifted confectioners' sugar
100 g/4 oz plain flour	1 cup all-purpose flour
50 g/2 oz cornflour	½ cup cornstarch
grated rind of 1 large lemon	grated rind of 1 large lemon
little caster sugar	little sugar

Fit the METAL BLADE. Put the butter and icing (confectioners') sugar in the bowl and process until light and fluffy.

Sift the flour and cornflour (cornstarch) and put in the bowl with the lemon rind. Process until the mixture has formed a smooth paste. Wrap the dough in cling film (plastic wrap) and chill until it is firm enough to handle. Shape the dough (paste) into a roll about 5 cm/2 inch in diameter. Wrap again in cling film (plastic wrap) then foil and chill well.

Roll the dough in the sugar and cut into 6 mm/¼ inch slices. Place on greased baking sheets, leaving 5 cm/2 inch between each. Bake in a moderately hot oven (190°C/375°F, Gas Mark 4) for 7 to 8 minutes or until the edges are golden. Loosen the crispies, if necessary, but leave to cool on the sheet to ensure maximum crispness.
Makes about 30 crispies
Note: The unbaked dough (paste) can be frozen. Wrap securely in foil. Before slicing, leave at room temperature for 10 minutes to soften slightly.

COFFEE OATEN BISCUITS (COOKIES)

Metric/Imperial	American
50 g/2 oz plain flour	½ cup all-purpose flour
pinch of bicarbonate of soda	pinch of baking soda
pinch of salt	pinch of salt
150 g/5 oz porridge oats	1½ cups porridge oats
100 g/4 oz butter	½ cup butter
50 g/2 oz caster sugar	4 tablespoons sugar
1 tablespoon golden syrup	1 tablespoon maple syrup
FILLING:	FILLING:
40 g/1½ oz butter	3 tablespoons butter
75 g/3 oz icing sugar, sifted	¾ cup sifted confectioners' sugar
coffee essence, to taste	strong black coffee, to taste
ICING:	FROSTING:
100 g/4 oz icing sugar, sifted	1 cup sifted confectioners' sugar
coffee essence, to taste	strong black coffee, to taste
boiling water, to mix	boiling water to mix

Sift the flour, soda and salt and mix with the oats.

Fit the PLASTIC BLADE. Put the butter, sugar and syrup in the bowl and process for 10 seconds. Add the oat mixture and combine, using 4 bursts of pulse action. Turn the dough (paste) onto a floured surface and roll out until 5 mm/¼ inch thick. Cut into rounds with a floured 5 cm/2 inch cutter. Place on greased baking sheets and bake in a moderate oven (160°C/325°F, Gas Mark 3) for about 15 to 20 minutes or until golden. Cool on the sheet.

Make the filling. Put the butter and sugar into the bowl and process until light. Remove to a small bowl and flavour with coffee essence (strong black coffee). Spread half the biscuits (cookies) with the filling and sandwich together, with the unspread biscuits (cookies).

Prepare the icing (frosting). Place the icing (confectioners') sugar in a small bowl, add a little coffee essence (strong black coffee) and mix to a thick spreading consistency. Beat with a wooden spoon, adding a very little boiling water. The icing (frosting) should drop from the spoon. Put a teaspoonful onto each paired biscuit (cookie) and leave to set.

Makes approximately 20 biscuits (cookies)

SCONES (BISCUITS)

Metric/Imperial	American
50 g/2 oz butter or margarine	¼ cup butter or margarine
225 g/8 oz plain flour	2 cups all-purpose flour
4 teaspoons baking powder	4 teaspoons baking powder
½ teaspoon salt	½ teaspoon salt
approximately 150 ml/¼ pint milk	approximately ⅔ cup milk

Fit the PLASTIC BLADE. Place the butter or margarine, flour, baking powder and salt in the processor bowl. Process to coarse breadcrumb stage, about 30 seconds. Pour in the milk and use pulse action to blend the mixture until a soft ball forms around the blade. Add more milk if the mixture looks dry.

Turn out the mixture onto a light floured surface and pat out to about 2 cm/¾ inch thick. With a floured 5 cm/2 inch round cutter cut into rounds or use a knife and cut into triangle shapes.

Place on a greased, floured baking sheet and bake in a hot oven (230°C/450°F, Gas Mark 8) for 8 to 10 minutes or until well risen and brown. Put on a rack and leave to cool.

Makes 10 to 12 scones (biscuits)

Variation

STANDBY SCONE (BISCUIT) MIX:
Blend the butter or margarine, flour, baking powder and salt in the food processor. Store in an airtight container in the refrigerator. Add the milk when needed.

ORANGE FRUIT SCONES (BISCUITS)

Metric/Imperial	American
225 g/8 oz self-raising flour	2 cups self-rising flour
1 teaspoon baking powder	1 teaspoon baking powder
50 g/2 oz butter	¼ cup butter
50 g/2 oz caster sugar	¼ cup sugar
grated rind of 1 orange	grated rind of 1 orange
75 g/3 oz currants	½ cup currants
150 ml/¼ pint milk	⅔ cup milk

Fit the PLASTIC BLADE. Place the flour, baking powder, butter, sugar and orange rind in the bowl and process for 10 seconds. Add the currants and milk and process until the mixture just forms a ball, about 15 seconds. Turn the paste onto a floured surface and roll out lightly to about 2 cm/¾ inch thickness. Cut out rounds with a floured 5 cm/2 inch cutter. Brush the tops with a little milk. Place on a lightly greased baking sheet. Cook in a hot oven (220°C/425°F, Gas Mark 7) until golden about 12 minutes.

Makes about 12 scones (biscuits)

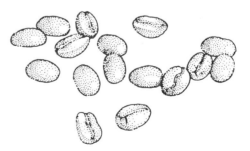

ENTERTAINING

Relaxing with friends, sharing experiences, getting to know people and occasionally spoiling the family, are entertaining at its best. Prepare a meal you have confidence in and are familiar with, rather than choose an elaborate new recipe that keeps you in the kitchen all evening. Most people have to consider the problems of preparing and serving the meal single handed so do as much advance preparation as you can, including setting the table, organising china and glasses and arranging flowers.

The food processor can be used to great advantage when entertaining; either completely prepare a dish so it is ready to serve or partly prepare a dish, so it is ready to assemble when necessary.

If you are a 'new' entertaining cook, plan a menu that is not all hot. Serve a cold dessert and easily made starter and a main course that will not spoil if kept waiting. Do remember that even the most organized cooks have disasters.

If the unexpected does happen and your main course burns, or your dessert is dropped on the floor and shatters to mix with the broken plate, all is not lost. The food processor can be used to turn out a speedy last-minute dish. A fruit pie can be specially prepared with pastry and sliced apples or canned pears. See the short cut and multiple meals chapter for further ideas. Pancakes (crêpes) with a savoury filling can be quickly prepared as can other face-saving dishes.

Whether friends drop in unexpectedly or the meal is planned, entertaining·is great fun. It is also the opportunity to use the 'best' of everything, including your food processor.

Apricot Punch (page 117)

DARIOLES ST GERMAIN

Metric/Imperial	American
40 g/1½ oz butter	3 tablespoons butter
40 g/1½ oz flour	3 tablespoons flour
175 ml/6 fl oz milk, scalded	¾ cup milk, scalded
350 g/12 oz frozen peas, defrosted and drained	¾ lb frozen peas, defrosted and drained
4 teaspoons gelatine	4 teaspoons unflavored gelatin
4 tablespoons medium sherry	4 tablespoons medium sherry
120 ml/4 fl oz strong chicken stock	½ cup strong chicken stock
salt	salt
freshly ground black pepper	freshly ground black pepper
250 ml/8 fl oz double cream, whipped	1 cup heavy cream, whipped
tomato and prawn sauce (page 48), to serve	tomato and shrimp sauce (page 48), to serve

Melt the butter and, when foaming, stir in the flour. Cook, stirring, for 2 minutes. Stir in the scalded milk and bring to the boil, stirring all the time. Simmer for 5 minutes. Fit the METAL BLADE.

Pour the sauce into the bowl and add the peas. Process until smooth, then pour into a large bowl. Sprinkle the gelatine over the sherry and leave to swell. Heat the stock to boiling point and pour onto the gelatine, stir until dissolved. Mix into the pea sauce, add salt and pepper to taste and fold in the cream. Pour the mixture into 6 individual wetted moulds, then chill until set. Turn onto salad dishes and serve with Tomato and Prawn (Shrimp) Sauce.
Serves 6

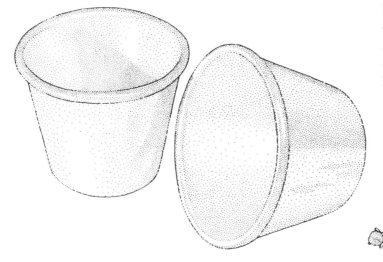

TIMBALES OF DUCK

Metric/Imperial	American
3 slices fresh brown bread, crusts removed	3 slices fresh brown bread, crusts removed
150 ml/¼ pint milk	⅔ cup milk
225 g/8 oz cooked duck trimmings	½ lb cooked duck trimmings
2 tablespoons sherry	2 tablespoons sherry
1 small onion, peeled and quartered	1 small onion, peeled and quartered
1 tablespoon parsley heads	1 tablespoon parsley heads
salt	salt
freshly ground black pepper	freshly ground black pepper
grated nutmeg	grated nutmeg
ground cloves	ground cloves
3 egg whites	3 egg whites
sprigs of watercress, to garnish	sprigs of watercress, to garnish
TO SERVE:	TO SERVE:
creamed spinach	creamed spinach
potato croquettes	potato croquettes
Sauce Valoise (page 49)	Sauce Valoise (page 49)

Fit the METAL BLADE. Break the bread into pieces and put into the bowl. Process until fine crumbs. Place the crumbs in a small pan, add the milk and cook very gently until the mixture looks granular. Place the duck, sherry, onion and parsley into the bowl and process until coarsely chopped. Add the bread mixture, salt, pepper, nutmeg and cloves. Process until finely chopped. Adjust the seasoning and place in a large bowl.

Whisk the egg whites until stiff but not dry and fold into the duck mixture. Divide between 4 buttered individual moulds leaving room to rise. Stand in a baking tin (pan) of hot water. Bake in a moderate oven (180°C/350°F, Gas Mark 4) for 30 minutes. Allow to stand for a few minutes before turning onto a heated serving dish. Serve with creamed spinach, potato croquettes and Sauve Valoise.
Serves 4

QUENELLES OF TUNA WITH TARRAGON SAUCE

Metric/Imperial	American
2 thick slices of white bread, crusts removed	2 thick slices of white bread, crusts removed
5 tablespoons milk	1/3 cup milk
1 × 200 g/7 oz can of tuna, drained	1 × 7 oz can of tuna, drained
50 g/2 oz butter, cut into pieces	1/4 cup butter, cut into pieces
1 egg	1 egg
3 large egg whites	3 large egg whites
freshly grated nutmeg	freshly grated nutmeg
salt	salt
freshly ground black pepper	freshly ground black pepper
SAUCE:	SAUCE:
2 sprigs of tarragon, leaves only or 1/2 teaspoon dried	2 sprigs of tarragon, leaves only or 1/2 teaspoon dried
2 small onions, peeled and quartered	2 small onions, peeled and quartered
25 g/1 oz butter	2 tablespoons butter
25 g/1 oz plain flour	1/4 cup all-purpose flour
150 ml/1/4 pint dry white wine	2/3 cup dry white wine
150 ml/1/4 pint chicken stock	2/3 cup chicken stock
squeeze of lemon juice	squeeze of lemon juice
salt	salt
freshly ground black pepper	freshly ground black pepper
150 ml/1/4 pint double cream	2/3 cup heavy cream
TO GARNISH:	TO GARNISH:
parsley	parsley

Fit the METAL BLADE. Break the bread into pieces and put in the bowl. Process to fine crumbs. Bring the milk to the boil in a small pan, add the crumbs, reduce the heat and beat with a wooden spoon until the mixture leaves the side of the pan. Spread into a greased shallow dish, cover with cling film (plastic wrap) and chill.

Put the tuna, butter, egg and egg whites, nutmeg, salt and pepper into the bowl. Process until smooth, add the milk mixture and process again until light. Return to the shallow dish, cover and chill. Wash the processor bowl.

Three-quarters fill a large saucepan with cold water. Bring to the boil, add salt and reduce to a simmer. Dip two dessertspoons in hot water and shape the mixture passing it from one spoon to the other. Drop the quenelles into the water and poach gently for 15 minutes, turning them over gently until they are puffed and set. Lift out carefully with a slotted spoon onto paper towels to drain. Arrange in a heated serving dish. Keep warm.

Prepare the sauce. Put the tarragon and onions into the bowl and process until finely chopped. Melt the butter in a pan and add the onion mixture and cook gently for 5 minutes. Stir in the flour and cook for 2 minutes. Gradually whisk in the wine, stock and lemon juice and bring to the boil. Add the salt and pepper to taste and stir in the cream. Mix well. Pour over the quenelles. Dust with a little parsley which has been chopped in the processor.

Serves 6

VITELLO TONNATO

Metric/Imperial	American
40 g/1½ oz butter	3 tablespoons butter
1.25 kg/2½ lb fillet of veal	2½ lb roasting veal
salt	salt
freshly ground black pepper	freshly ground black pepper
300 ml/½ pint mayonnaise (page 48)	1¼ cups mayonnaise (page 48)
1 × 75 g/3 oz can of tuna, drained	1 × 3 oz can of tuna, drained
2 tablespoons capers	2 tablespoons capers
TO GARNISH:	TO GARNISH:
¼ cucumber, peeled	¼ cucumber, peeled
black olives, pitted	ripe olives, pitted

Spread the butter over the veal and season with salt and pepper. Wrap in a large piece of foil. Place in a roasting tin (pan) and cook in a moderate oven (160 C/325 F, Gas Mark 3), allowing 45 minutes per 450 g/1 lb. Open the foil and baste from time to time. Allow to cool completely.

Fit the PLASTIC BLADE. Put the mayonnaise and tuna into the bowl and process until smooth. Add 2 tablespoons of the meat juices and use pulse action to blend. Adjust seasoning then wash the bowl.

Slice the veal and arrange on a serving dish. Pour over the tuna sauce and sprinkle with the capers.

Fit the SLICING DISC and use to slice the cucumber. Arrange the slices around the dish in twists. Tuck an olive into every twist.

Serves 8

STUFFED PORK FILLET

Metric/Imperial	American
3 large onions, peeled and quartered	3 large onions, peeled and quartered
1 tablespoon olive oil	1 tablespoon olive oil
2 slices wholemeal bread, crusts removed	2 slices wholewheat bread, crusts removed
small handful parsley, washed and dried	small handful parsley, washed and dried
175 g/6 oz pork sausage meat or 175 g/6 oz piece belly pork	¾ cup (6 oz) pork sausage meat or 6 oz piece of fatty pork
salt	salt
freshly ground black pepper	freshly ground black pepper
½ teaspoon fennel seeds	½ teaspoon fennel seeds
1 head celery	1 bunch celery
2 pork fillets, about 275–300 g/10–12 oz each	2 pork tenderloins, about 10–12 oz each
25 g/1 oz butter or margarine	2 tablespoons butter or margarine
150 ml/¼ pint stock	⅔ cup stock
4 tablespoons single cream	¼ cup light cream

Fit the METAL BLADE. Finely chop 1 of the onions. Heat the oil in a large frying pan (skillet), add the onion and cook until soft but not brown. Remove from the heat. Break the bread into pieces and process to fine crumbs, remove. Finely chop the parsley and add with the crumbs to the onion.

If using belly of pork (fatty pork), process until finely minced. Add the sausage meat or minced pork, salt, pepper and fennel seeds to the pan. Stir well and cook lightly until the meat is browned, set aside.

Fit the SLICING DISC. Slice the remaining onions and the celery. Split each pork fillet down the centre, almost all the way through, and flatten out with a rolling pin or meat mallet. Spread the stuffing on one flattened fillet and lay the other on top. Press and skewer together with cocktail sticks (toothpicks).

Melt the butter or margarine in a large frying pan (skillet) and brown the pork on both sides, turning carefully. Remove and set aside. In the same fat, sauté the sliced onion and celery for about 5 minutes, stirring often. Put the onion and celery in a casserole dish and lay the pork on top. Heat the stock with salt and pepper to taste and pour over the pork. Cover and bake in a moderate oven (180 C/350 F, Gas Mark 4) for 45 to 60 minutes.

Place the pork on a wooden board, remove the cocktail sticks (toothpicks), and slice the meat. Place the onion and celery on a serving dish and put the meat slices on top. Keep warm.

Pour the juices from the casserole into a small pan and bring to the boil. Stir in cream and simmer over a low heat (do not allow to boil) for about 3 minutes or until well reduced. Serve in a sauce boat.

Serves 4 to 6

From left: Burgundy Velvet (page 116) and Vitello Tonnato

LAMB CHOPS WITH SORREL

Metric/Imperial	American
6 lamb chops, cut 2.5 cm/ 1 inch thick	6 lamb chops, cut 1 inch thick
25 g/1 oz butter	2 tablespoons butter
little oil	little oil
1 small onion, peeled	1 small onion, peeled
225 g/8 oz sorrel leaves, washed and shaken dry	8 oz sorrel leaves, washed and shaken dry
120 ml/4 fl oz white wine	½ cup white wine
few fresh mint leaves	few fresh mint leaves
120 ml/4 fl oz double cream	½ cup heavy cream
salt	salt
freshly ground black pepper	freshly ground black pepper
watercress sprigs, to garnish	watercress sprigs, to garnish

Trim the fat from the chops. Melt the butter in a frying pan (skillet) and add the oil. Cook the chops for 3 minutes on each side, do not overcook. Fit the SLICING DISC and use to slice the onion. Keep the chops warm on a heated serving dish.

Pour away all but 1 tablespoon of the fat in the pan (skillet). Add the onion and cook for 5 minutes. Stir in the sorrel, wine and mint. Cook over a high heat until the sorrel wilts and the liquid is reduced to a few tablespoons. Fit the METAL BLADE.

Pour the sorrel mixture into the bowl and process until smooth. Return to a small pan and stir in the cream. Add salt and pepper and bring to the boil. Reduce the heat and simmer for a few minutes. Pour over the chops and garnish with watercress.

Serves 4

BURGUNDY VELVET

Metric/Imperial	American
6 egg yolks	6 egg yolks
75 g/3 oz caster sugar	6 tablespoons sugar
4 tablespoons burgundy	4 tablespoons burgundy
grated rind of 1 lemon	grated rind of 1 lemon
2 tablespoons lemon juice	2 tablespoons lemon juice
1 tablespoon brandy	1 tablespoon brandy
TO DECORATE AND SERVE:	TO DECORATE AND SERVE:
6 purple grapes, sliced	6 black grapes, sliced
sponge fingers	ladyfingers

Fit the PLASTIC BLADE. Put the egg yolks and sugar into the bowl and process until thick and light. Add the burgundy, lemon rind and juice and brandy and process until blended. Pour the mixture into the top of a double boiler or a heatproof bowl placed over a pan of simmering water. Whisk continually until the mixture holds a peak. Remove from the heat and allow to cool a little. Pour into six stemmed wine glasses and decorate with the grapes. Serve immediately with sponge fingers (ladyfingers).
Serves 6

RUM AND COCONUT ICE CREAM

Metric/Imperial	American
1 coconut, shelled, broken into pieces and peeled	1 coconut, shelled, broken into pieces and peeled
350 ml/12 fl oz double cream	1½ cups heavy cream
450 ml/¾ pint milk	2 cups milk
6 egg yolks	6 egg yolks
225 g/8 oz caster sugar	1 cup sugar
3 tablespoon dark rum, or to taste	3 tablespoons dark rum, or to taste
TO SERVE:	TO SERVE:
bananas baked in rum, butter and brown sugar	bananas baked in rum, butter and brown sugar

Fit the GRATING DISC. Pack the coconut into the feed tube and grate.

In a large heavy pan, combine the grated coconut, cream and milk. Bring slowly to scalding point but do not allow to boil. Remove from the heat and leave to infuse for about 30 minutes.

Line a fine sieve with muslin (cheesecloth), which has been wrung out in cold water. Strain the coconut liquid into a bowl, gather up the cloth and squeeze out the remaining liquid. Discard the coconut, and wash the pan.

Fit the METAL BLADE. Put the egg yolks and sugar into the bowl and process until thick and light. Pour the coconut milk through the feed tube and process until well blended. Pour into the washed pan and cook over a gentle heat, stirring constantly, until the custard coats the back of a wooden spoon. Do not allow the custard to boil. Gradually stir in the rum, tasting as you go. (More can be added if liked.) Cover with cling film (plastic wrap) and leave to cool. Pour into a metal container and freeze. Beat the mixture once or twice during freezing, to break down the ice crystals. This can be done in the processor using the plastic blade. Serve with baked bananas.
Serves 8

COFFEE HAZELNUT MOUSSE

Metric/Imperial	American
175 g/6 oz hazelnuts	1 cup hazelnuts
4 egg yolks	4 egg yolks
175 g/6 oz caster sugar	¾ cup sugar
2 teaspoons instant coffee powder	2 teaspoons instant coffee powder
1 teaspoon vanilla essence	1 teaspoon vanilla extract
300 ml/½ pint double cream	1¼ cups heavy cream
TO DECORATE:	TO DECORATE:
whipped cream	whipped cream
6 toasted hazelnuts	6 toasted hazelnuts
TO SERVE:	TO SERVE:
Chocolate Brandy Sauce (page 55)	Chocolate Brandy Sauce (page 55)

Put the nuts on a baking sheet and toast in a moderate oven (180°C//350°F, Gas Mark 4) for about 12 minutes or until they are golden. Wrap the nuts in a teatowel, leave for a few moments, then rub them hard to remove the skins. Reserve 6 of the best nuts.

Fit the METAL BLADE. When the nuts are cool, put them into the bowl and process until finely ground. Set aside.

Fit the PLASTIC BLADE. Place the yolks, sugar, coffee and vanilla into the bowl and process until thick and light, scraping down the bowl once or twice. Whip the cream in a large chilled bowl until stiff, then fold

in the egg and sugar mixture, and nuts. Oil six individual china ramekins. Spoon in the mousse and cover with cling film (plastic wrap), chill. To serve, run a thin-bladed knife around the edge of the dishes and turn carefully onto plates. Decorate with a rosette of whipped cream topped with a hazelnut. Accompany with cold Chocolate Brandy Sauce.
Serves 6

SIMPLE TRUFFLES

Metric/Imperial	American
225 g/8 oz stale chocolate or coffee cake, cut into slices	½ lb stale chocolate or coffee cake, cut into slices
50 g/2 oz ground almonds	½ cup ground almonds
25 g/1 oz soft brown sugar	1½ tablespoons light brown sugar
1 tablespoon apricot jam	1 tablespoon apricot jelly
1 tablespoon rum or ½ teaspoon rum essence	1 tablespoon rum or ½ teaspoon rum extract
75 g/3 oz plain chocolate	3 squares semi-sweet chocolate
50 g/2 oz chocolate vermicelli	½ cup chocolate sprinkles

Fit the PLASTIC BLADE. Put the cake, almonds, sugar, jam (jelly) and rum into the bowl and process until it forms a ball around the blade. Melt the chocolate in a small bowl over hot water. Roll the cake mixture into balls the size of a walnut. Coat with the melted chocolate, remove and drain, then roll in the vermicelli
Makes about 20 truffles

STRAWBERRY DAIQUARI

Metric/Imperial	American
275 g/10 oz fresh or frozen, defrosted strawberries	2 cups fresh or frozen, defrosted strawberries
250 ml/8 fl oz white rum	1 cup white rum
1 tablespoon lemon juice	1 tablespoon lemon juice
2 teaspoons grenadine	2 teaspoons grenadine
4 marashino cherries, on sticks, to decorate	4 marashino cherries, on sticks, to decorate

Fit the METAL BLADE. Place all the ingredients, except the cherries, into the bowl. Process until smooth.
Half-fill four chilled goblets with crushed ice and fill up with Daiquari. Decorate each glass with a cherry.
Serves 4

APRICOT PUNCH

Metric/Imperial	American
225 g/8 oz dried apricots, soaked overnight	1¼ cups dried apricots, soaked overnight
100 g/4 oz sugar	½ cup sugar
250 ml/8 fl oz orange juice	1 cup orange juice
juice of 1 large lemon	juice of 1 large lemon
250 ml/8 fl oz sweet cider	1 cup sweet hard cider
soda water, to serve	soda water, to serve
TO DECORATE:	TO DECORATE:
sprigs of borage or mint	sprigs of borage or mint
glacé cherries	candied cherries

Simmer the apricots and the soaking liquid with the sugar until tender. Fit the PLASTIC BLADE.
Place the apricots and liquid in the bowl and process until smooth. Combine the orange and lemon juice and cider in a large bowl and stir in the apricot mixture. Chill.
For each serving, fill a tumbler one-third full with apricot punch. Top with soda water and decorate with a borage or mint sprig and a cherry on a stick.
Serves 8 to 10

SHORT CUT
INGREDIENTS &
MULTIPLE MEALS

Are you familiar with that recurring dream, in which you return home after an exhausting day, to find a delicious home cooked meal awaiting you? Or the fantasy in which you calmly serve a superb dinner to unexpected guests, undeterred by the usual domestic chaos reigning in the background? Use your processor and, with reorganization and some experimenting, this can become a reality.

There are two ways to benefit from the labour-saving technique of making more than one dish at a time.

First, there are items called for so regularly that it is practical to have them ready processed on hand any time they're needed. These are all 'short cut ingredients', processed in bulk and stored for later use, to enliven your cooking and add to your convenience.

Second, there are 'multiple meals' or 'chain cooking' – complete dishes made with similar ingredients at one session. Use this method to assemble several dishes and cut down on kitchen mess.

In planning a chain, the right balance between dishes that can be stored and those to be enjoyed at once is crucial if you want to avoid cycles of feast and famine. Do remember though, that although a completed dish may not store very well, often certain processed foodstuffs that go into it fall into the 'short cut ingredients' category, so make them up in advance during a session of chain cooking, and store them until needed. You can then assemble 'non storables' very easily, using prepared ingredients.

A selection of short cut
ingredients

SHORT CUT INGREDIENTS

A short cut ingredient is any item frequently used in the kitchen, perhaps a little fiddly to make and which can be processed in bulk and stored until needed. The following suggestions will be useful time and again.

Chopped onion crops up almost daily; why not chop a large quantity and freeze? Breadcrumbs are invaluable for stuffings, coatings and toppings, and can be stored frozen or in an airtight container.

Biscuit crumbs made from digestive biscuits (Graham crackers) or ginger biscuits (snaps) are good for quick dessert treats. With melted butter the ginger crumbs can be made into a pie crust; add Crème Pâtissière (page 54) and canned apricots for an instant apricot ginger tart.

A large quantity of homemade Mayonnaise can be made into many varied sauces with simple additions processed into it (see page 48). The processor combines these in seconds and they add the finishing touch which makes a meal something special.

Biscuit (cookie) dough can be made in bulk and frozen in cylindrical shapes; simply slice off as many as you need and bake.

Croûtons are a lovely crisp addition to soups, and are made by chopping slightly stale bread in the machine, frying until crisp, draining well and freezing or storing in an airtight container.

Wash and dry fresh herbs then finely chop in the processor. Place in ice cube trays, covered with water and freeze. Chopped dried fruits and nuts are handy for baking or try orange and lemon essences (extracts); these are made by processing strips of orange or lemon peel (no pith) until finely chopped. Cover with vodka and leave for six weeks.

Bacon leftovers can be processed finely and, when cooked, will freeze well, for a crunchy addition to salads or sandwich fillings or use as a garnish.

Casserole vegetables or soup mixes
Make a beef pot roast or casserole with speedily sliced celery, onions and carrots. Slice an extra amount and put on for soup or freeze, ready for soup.

Basic meat mixture
Minced (ground) meat can be made into a basic usable portions and freeze. Use as liked.

Fit the metal blade. Finely mince (grind) 550 g/1¼ lb cubed lean beef. Set aside. Chop 1 carrot. Heat 1 tablespoon oil and cook 1 clove crushed garlic until fragrant. Add the beef, carrot, 1 × 400 g/14 oz can tomatoes, 1 teaspoon dried mixed herbs, 2 teaspoons celery seeds and salt and pepper to taste. Simmer for 30 minutes. Cool, label and freeze.

Pastry
Pastry is ideal for chain or short cut cookups as it feeezes well and can be used in so many different guises. Any of the pastry recipes given on pages 100 or 101 can be stored frozen, prior to rolling out, or made into pie shells and frozen, baked blind, or raw uncooked.

To save time, pastry can be frozen in circles cut to fit a pie dish, and the filling frozen in just the correct quantity and shape to fit the dish used.

Butters
The food processor creams butters in seconds, simply inviting the addition of herbs, garlic, icing (confectioners') sugar, orange juice and rind or liqueur and sugar – the list is almost endless.

TO MAKE SAVOURY BUTTER Fit the metal blade and process 225 g/8 oz/2 sticks butter until creamy. Add any of the following suggestions: 3 cloves garlic, crushed; 4–6 tablespoons finely chopped parsley plus a little lemon juice or 4 tablespoons finely chopped mint. For Special Herbed Butter process ½ small onion, 1 clove garlic, 2 sprigs parsley and a pinch each fresh thyme and tarragon until finely chopped. Add 225 g/8 oz/2 sticks butter, 1 teaspoon prepared mustard, ½ teaspoon cognac and 1 egg yolk to the bowl. Process until well combined and smooth.

Carefully remove the savoury butter mixture from the blades and gently roll into a cylindrical shape. Wrap well in cling film (plastic wrap) and foil and freeze or refrigerate. Slice off as much as is needed, using a knife dipped in hot water.

Use savoury butters for grilled (broiled) or roasted meats, cooked vegetables or to spread on French bread.
TO MAKE BUTTER CREAM Fit the metal blade and process 225 g/8 oz/2 sticks of butter until creamy. Add 350 g/12 oz/2²/3 cups sifted icing (confectioners') sugar and process until light and fluffy. Flavour with melted chocolate or cocoa powder, strong black coffee, orange or lemon juices, rum or brandy.

Use butter creams to fill and ice (frost) a plain cake or to serve with steamed puddings.

If you are following the idea of short cut ingredients you will be able to add your own ideas as well. When you use part of your store of short cuts do remember to process more to replace what you have used. It is not necessary to do this right on the spot, as this is why the short cut ingredients are there, but do try to replace within a couple of days.

MULTIPLE MEALS OR CHAIN COOKING

What triggers off a chain and how do you put one together? There are a few tricks to it.

A common 'trigger' is a seasonal glut, or a favourite fruit or vegetable becoming available at a lower price. You can take advantage of these savings with tremendous variety.

The idea is to find the common denominator in dishes you would like to make, and then to simplify things by doing the processing for more than one in a single session.

Apples are marvellously versatile, and if you have a large crop or buy them by the caseful, you might be wondering what to do with them. Apples freeze well, either by themselves or mixed with other ingredients, or they can be made into apple sauce.

An apple chain can be made up from some of the following suggestions, or use your own receipes. See the Shortcut ingredients, at left, as some of the suggestions can be used in this chain.

Waldorf Salad

Fit the metal blade and use to chop 50 g/2 oz/½ cup walnuts. Remove and put in a bowl. Peel and core 450 g/1 lb apples and coarsely chop in the processor. Remove and put with the walnuts. Fit the slicing disc and use to slice 2 sticks celery. Add to the walnuts. Add enough well-flavoured Mayonnaise (page 48) to moisten. Refrigerate for up to 2 days.

Serves 4

Apple stuffing

Remove the crusts from 450 g/1 lb 2-day old wholewheat bread and break into pieces. Fit the metal blade and process the bread into crumbs. Spread on a baking tray and dry out in a slow oven.

Wash and dry a handful of parsley and process until finely chopped, remove. Process 1 large stick celery and 1 peeled onion until finely chopped. Sauté the onion and celery in 50 g/2 oz/2 tablespoons butter until golden. Meanwhile, peel and core 8 cooking (baking) apples and process to small dice. Add to the onion mixture with 175 g/6 oz/1 cup brown sugar, ½ teaspoon each dried sage, marjoram and thyme; and salt and pepper to taste. Cook for a few minutes, stirring to cook evenly. Pour over the dried crumbs in a bowl and mix evenly. Freeze or use immediately for duck or pork.

Apple and ham bake

Fit the metal blade. Remove the crusts from 2 slices of white bread, break into pieces and process to fine crumbs. Remove and set aside. Process 2 slices cooked, smoked ham (sliced 1.5 cm/¾ inch thick then cut into pieces) with ½ an onion peeled, until coarsely chopped. Add ¼ teaspoon ground cloves, salt and pepper to taste, ½ teaspoon dry mustard, 1 egg and 120 ml/4 fl oz/½ cup milk. Process, using pulse action, until combined. Put into a shallow ovenproof dish, patting down lightly.

Peel and core 350 g/12 oz/¾ lb eating apples. Fit the slicing disc and slice the apples. Arrange on top of the ham mixture and drizzle over 2 to 4 tablespoons honey (depending on taste). Dot with 25 g/1 oz/2 tablespoons butter. Bake in a moderately hot oven (190°C/375°F, Gas Mark 5) for 40 minutes.

If you plan to follow this apple chain, it is a sensible idea to make a shopping list and organize yourself to do the cooking at one session. If you have more apples than you want to make into dishes, they freeze very well. Refer to a freezer book for the correct way to prepare and freeze apples. The apples can then be easily removed and popped into a frozen pastry shell for an easy dessert.

Once you become familiar with the idea of multiple meals and chain cooking, work out your own ideas.

Courgettes (zucchini) and leeks make a good chain and run onto each other. For example, Courgette (Zucchini) flan starts off a chain of ideas which in turn leads to a leek chain. Ratatouille is a versatile vegetable combination and equally delicious served hot or cold. Courgettes (Zucchini) Parmesan, sautéed in butter with chopped shallots and a sprinkling of grated Parmesan and breadcrumbs are subtle and light while Courgette (Zucchini) and leek soup can lead to a session of Vichyssoise from which watercress can be added to make Watercress soup.

The soups and flan in the above chain can be frozen and ratatouille will keep well in the refrigerator. Remember to make your shopping list and cook at one session.

A dairy chain is also rewarding, and can consist of ice cream, cheesecake, Crème Pâtissière and pancake (crêpe) batter. (All the recipes are in the book.)

Mushrooms and cheese can be made into a chain as can many other ingredients. The processor is very rewarding when working in a chain and a little thought, advance preparation and a few days cooking will see you through busy weekends.

INDEX

NOTES

The recipes in this book have been tested using a Pifco
food processor. If you have a different food processor,
follow the manufacturer's leaflet.

- All recipes serve 4 unless otherwise stated
- Ovens should be preheated to the specified temperature
- All spoon measures are level
- Metric spoon measures in sizes 1.25 ml
  ($\frac{1}{4}$ teaspoon), 2.5 ml ($\frac{1}{2}$ teaspoon, 5 ml (1 teaspoon) and
  15 ml (1 tablespoon) are available and should be used
  for accurate measurement of small quantities
- Follow only one column of ingredients, they are not
  interchangeable.
- Follow only one set of measures, either metric or
  imperial or American; they are not interchangeable.

NOTES FOR AUSTRALIAN USERS

All measurements in this book are given in metric, imperial
and American. In Australia, the 250 ml metric measuring
cup is used. The set of graduated cups should be used for
measuring dry ingredients and the litre jug or 250 ml cup
should be used for measuring liquid ingredients. If
Australian users follow the American column they should
remember that the American pint is 16 fl oz (equivalent to
2 cups).

It is important to note that the Australian tablespoon
has been converted to 20 ml, which is larger than the
tablespoon used in all columns in this book and, therefore,
3 level teaspoons should be used where instructed to use 1
tablespoon. Kitchen scales may be used to follow either the
metric or imperial columns but only one set of measures
should be used, they are not interchangeable.

ACKNOWLEDGMENTS

Special photography by Roger Phillips
Jacket photograph by Theo Bergström
Food for photography prepared by Valerie Barret
Illustrations by Elsa Willson
Chapter heading illustrations by Isobel Balakrishnan